MUCH MORE
EARLY AMERICAN PATTERN GLASS

ALICE HULETT METZ

COLLECTOR BOOKS
A Division of Schroeder Publishing Co., Inc.

The current values of this book should be used only as a guide. They are not intended to set prices, which vary from one section of the country to another. Auction prices as well as dealer prices vary and are affected by condition as well as demand. Neither the author nor the publisher assumes responsibility for any losses that might be incurred as a result of consulting this guide.

Front cover: Glass provided by Irving and June Terzich.
#1285 Bullet Emblem Covered Sugar, $350.00

Cover design by **Beth Summers**
Book design by **Ben Faust**

Searching for a Publisher?

We are always looking for knowledgeable people considered to be experts within their fields. If you feel there is a real need for a book on your collectible subject and have a large comprehensive collection, contact Collector Books.

COLLECTOR BOOKS
P.O. Box 3009
Paducah, Kentucky 42002-3009

www.collectorbooks.com

Copyright © 2000 by Judith Cronin

FOREWORD

This revision of *Much More Early American Pattern Glass* is the work of a committee made up of volunteers from the Early American Pattern Glass Society. The society felt that the Metz books needed to be back in print and found that the publisher, Collector Books, was willing to reissue them if the price guides were revised and other changes made. It was more than two years between proposal and publication. The input of many people across the United States contributed to this edition. I want to thank the committee: Walt and Linda Adams of Minnesota, Robert Burford of Rhode Island, Mary Haskell of Illinois, Kat Krivda of Ohio, San Kissee of California, Mel & Roberta Lader of Virginia, and Irving and June Terzich of California who contributed to revisions of sections of the book and reviewed the work of their fellow committee members. Also contributing to revisions of specific patterns, picking out Depression era glass from EAPG, auction records, and bibliographic materials were Jeff Evans of Green Valley Auctions, George Miller and Steven Skeim. I also want to thank Steven Skeim and the Terzichs for allowing their personal glass pieces to be photographed for the covers of both books. While we don't feel these are the definitive books on collecting Early American Pattern Glass, the numerous photographs and notes make them standard references for identifying it. Probably not all errors have been eliminated and we may have inadvertently added some of our own, but we tried to the best of our ability to keep the revisions factual based on current information and our years of experience in collecting and buying and selling. New discoveries in glass research come to light and render old work obsolete, but this only adds to the fascination of pattern glass. Although it was made 100 – 150 years ago, collectors can always discover something new about it.

Phyllis Petcoff
President and Committee Chair
Early American Pattern Glass Society

Judith Cronin, a well known dealer and collector of early American pattern glass since the 1960s, holds the copyright to this book and participated in revising the values contained herein. She resides in Orleans, Cape Cod, Massachusetts.

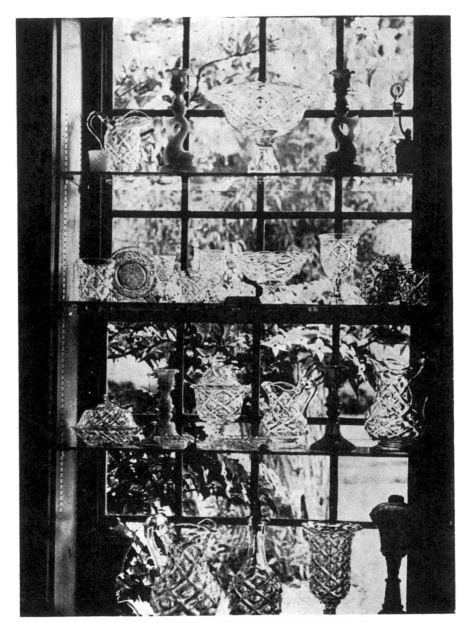

WINDOW OF SANDWICH MUSEUM.

PREFACE

J.M.J.

You may remember I launched my first book with the slogan, "Now only one book is needed etc." Then followed six booklets, and now I, who deplore exaggerated advertising claims come out with this, and from where I am now it looks as if my life will not be long enough to complete the story of pattern glass. And you, dear readers, are the ones, who wakened me to all the many questions and the many undiscovered worthwhile patterns and pieces in those patterns. It seems I never go to a show or visit a museum or a collection but I come away with some kernels of new knowledge or some new question or both. My mail is flooded with both. Shortly after my first book was issued, I sat in the kitchen of a lovely old home on Cape Cod which belonged to a collector. The window ledges were lined with tiny whisky tasters and mugs in patterns which I'd never seen nor which have not been listed. As I moved about the area I found goblets, spills, etc. The hunt was on. Here is the result.

It has been much work; a great deal of traveling was involved and needless to say, it has been time consuming. I wish I might have had more time checking some details further but a line must be drawn in a never ending task. It has been most rewarding. No one can ever tell me that this is not a world full of generous, helpful people.

Two years ago, when relations between the United States and Canada were slightly strained, I was invited there to open an antique show. I could not have been treated more kindly nor generously had I been visiting royalty. I owe much to Mrs. Mary Sutherland of *The Telegram* in Toronto, who, unknown to me, had reviewed my book on the air and in the press. The Hon. John Yaremko, hesitated, in the midst of a busy campaign, to get out his collection of glass for me to see. The Royal Museum's busy curator spent precious time unlocking cases for me to see glass. The Canadian press, the Canadian people were the friendliest in the world. How far from right were the newspaper headlines of the day!

Mr. and Mrs. Kenneth Wakefield are always ready to befriend the writer or student of antiques and their glorious collections were opened to me. Mrs. Wakefield, a director of the Sandwich Museum gives unselfishly of her time to that fine institution also.

Mr. and Mrs. Nicholson, of Chatham, Massachusetts, gave me freedom to picture their fine glass.

Mrs. Doris Kershaw, Curator of my beloved Sandwich Museum, who spent much time, removing glass from cases for us to picture. To the Sandwich Museum for the wonderful work it is doing in upholding American standards, all real Americans owe a debt.

Miss Marion Dana, a niece of Mr. Swan, who wrote the book on Portland Glass and opened her fine collection to me and shared her vast knowledge of that factory with me. To the Portland Museum for allowing us to picture their fine glass and handle these rare specimens.

Dr. and Mrs. Bruce Swift gave a collection of 1500 goblets to the Allen Art Museum in Oberlin, Ohio, where all may enjoy them; they deserve our thanks.

Mr. Harold Allen made the fine cover picture for me and he is always ready to help with pictures; clear photos mean much.

Many, many, too numerous to mention have sent me bits of information; glass to be pictured, some of these have led to important discoveries.

Above all thanks are due to the serious glass students who have used six large printings of my first book in the comparatively brief period of its existence. All I can say is I'll try not to disappoint you; many, many thanks,

Another glass student,
ALICE HULETT METZ

October, 1965

DEDICATION

To all those, who, like our American ancestors, can take pleasure and see beauty in the simple things of li
such as the weeds by the wayside, the flowers and fruits of the garden, the tall trees of the lanes and t
woods, and who can find humor in the most unexpected places and situations, and who, at all times, feel
deep reverence for the country of which these things are a part, this book is gratefully dedicated by

Just another American

ALICE HULETT METZ

760
Fern with Lily of
the Valley

785
Panelled Acorn Band

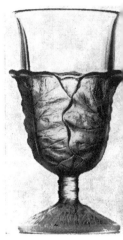

1156
Cabbage Leaf

166
Union Forever Mug

577
Clover

166
Union Forever Mug

6

1285
Bullet-Emblem

1084
Owl and Pussy Cat Cheese Dish

DEDICATION PAGE PATTERNS

No. 577 – CLOVER – L. 141 calls this STIPPLED CLOVER and shows the identical dish with stippled background. This one is in the SANDWICH MUSEUM. It has a background of tiny concentric circles of very fine lines. This is what may have been meant in the line drawing in Lee and this is the reason I prefer to use photos. It would have been almost impossible to draw the the texture of this background as it is. This butter has four leaf clovers in the base; it is very scarce but not in demand as collectors are not familiar with it. It is clear, non-flint of the 70s or early 80s. Goblets would be worth $75.00 as goblet collectors would like to have one. Wine $35.00; large plate $25.00; covered butter $65.00.

No. 760 – FERN WITH LILY-of-the-VALLEY – Listed but not pictured in my first book. Goblet now $45.00.

No. 785 – PANELLED ACORN BAND – Pitcher listed but not shown in first book. It and the creamer are shown here to show that some of the non-flint patterns possess all the beauty of some of the flint and to show the slight difference in the way the design is handled on the two pitchers. They may have been products of different factories. Water pitcher $95.00; creamer $45.00.

No. 1084 – OWL AND PUSSY CAT CHEESE DISH – I'm not too certain that this cheese dish is not a member of the TILE BAND pattern, covered on page 139, for it carries the same band of tile and in many patterns the platters and cheese dishes wax pictorial. It is well known by this name so why change to the more prosaic title. Rare $250.00.

No. 1156 – CABBAGE LEAF – Listed but not pictured in my first book. REPRODUCTION goblets, wines, champagnes, goblets in color now flooding the market. I've never seen a goblet, wine, champagne nor a colored piece in the pattern. In demand and scarce. Large compote, pictured $150.00; celery, pictured $90.00; tumbler $75.00; plate, bunny in center $65.00. *Stemware not part of original production. Pitcher, $250.00; covered sugar $125.00; butter $135.00; creamer $90.00.*

No. 166 – UNION FOREVER MUG – Flint Civil War mug, clear, made in Massachusetts in 1863. Also made in whiskey tumbler, handleless $375.00; mug $300.00. Scarce. On one side, "Union forever," on the reverse, "A bumper to the flag."

COVER PICTURE

No. 1285 – BULLET-EMBLEM – Clear, non-flint, made in 1898, a Spanish American War souvenir. In demand because of its historical interest. All I've ever seen are the spooners $125.00; covered butter $350.00; covered sugar $250.00; creamer $135.00. *75% more with good polychrome paint.*

7
Primitive

23
Pathfinder

25
Lobular Bull's Eye

62
Giant Bull's Eye

139
Bull's Eye and Cube

61
Flute with Bull's Eye

64
Bull's Eye and
Broken Column

13
Bull's Eye and Sawtooth

EARLIEST FLINT PATTERNS

Sturdiness is reflected in these patterns and I feel it was more than accidental. The pressing machine may have presented difficulties in removing fragile pieces from the mold and the process was still too new to reach the ease and perfection of later years. In these patterns little besides the goblets has been found in most of them but I believe that may be due to the fact that there would be a dozen goblets in a home as opposed to one creamer or sugar. Then, too, many of these have not been previously listed. I'm hoping that after this listing I'll hear of other pieces from readers. The full glass story will need the help of every one if it is ever to near completion.

No. 7 – PRIMITIVE – Not previously listed. From the Swift collection. Clear flint of the 40s. I'd say a goblet as old and scarce as this is worth from $50.00.

No. 23 – PATHFINDER – Previously unlisted. Form the Nickerson collection. Early flint, of the 40s, $75.00 – $100.00.

No. 25 – LOBULAR BULL'S EYE – Heretofore unlisted; Swift collection. Clear flint of the late 40s or early 50s. Goblet $210.00.

No. 62 – GIANT BULL'S EYE – Mil. Bk. 2 – 149. Clear flint of the 50s. Goblet $110.00; creamer $150.00.

No. 139 – BULL'S EYE AND CUBE – Not previously listed. Clear flint of late 40s. Goblet $150.00.

No. 61 – FLUTE WITH BULL'S EYE – Mil. – Bk. 2-154. Clear flint. Goblet $75.00; wine $50.00.

No. 64 – BULL'S EYE AND BROKEN COLUMN – Mil. – Bk. 2-30. Clear flint of the early 50s. Goblet $130.00; *footed tumbler $100.00 (see #60 P12).*

No. 13 – BULL'S EYE AND SAWTOOTH – Mil. – Bk. 2-30. Clear flint of the late 50s. Goblet $110.00.

HOW DO WE LEARN ABOUT OLD GLASS?

At last, I feel I may be able to explain to novices the way to go about the collecting hobby. My readers made it most plain to me today. A man called me in the morning and expected me to be able to give him the ability to choose between the desirable and the worthless over the phone. Evidently he was very sincere and while it is a physical impossibility for me to spend time with phone callers, his earnestness touched me and I tried to help him, "Read, study, go to good shows, buy a piece from a reputable dealer, read, study, more," was my theme song. Then he told me he went to country auctions over the weekends. I tried to convince him that these auctions were places where only people who really knew value found a rare prize. "Oh, I never pay more than two dollars for any piece of glass," he continued. I give up; I suggested he had better study more.

The day was as difficult as its beginning; we were preparing for two shows, mail orders were excessively heavy, I'm no longer in the bloom of youth. But along came a letter! A ship's captain, sailing the Great Lakes wrote me of his treasures. He knew what he had, he quoted the books in which they were listed. He had found some of them at auctions. They are not for sale; he treasures them. (Incidentally, my book rides the waves with him.)

This is the type of person who will find bargains, the one who enjoys knowing about them, knows values, and who can tell what glass will have a future. He is not led by the mob, is not a fad collector, nor a speculator.

Did I say the day was difficult? I meant different, delightful. Just think of the many people like that scattered over our fair land, even sailing our ships. I'm so glad they are there.

Some of these patterns may be English. They are found there frequently. British glass of the 1850s and 1860s was also flint, usually heavier, more block shaped, with shorter, thicker stems.

207
Framed Ovals

211
Framed **Blocks**

217
Ringed Frame Blocks

205
Panelled **Frames**

165
Terraced Bull's Eye

222
Oval Panelled Frames

220
Framed Circles

208
Ringed Frame Ovals

10

No. 207 – FRAMED OVALS – Fine, clear flint, gilt trimmed, of the 40s, possibly made at the Sandwich factory or its neighbor, the New England Glass Co. I believe many of the goblets shown on this page and the following page had their origin in either one of these factories as they and many pieces such as whiskey tasters and small vases are to be found in the treasures of the old homes in the vicinity. They are all, exceptionally fine, bell tones glass with all the ear marks of very early manufacture. $210.00.

No. 211 – FRAMED BLOCKS – Mil. Bk. 2-126. Clear flint, slightly later than some of the others, but obviously earlier than the 70s as listed by Dr. Millard. Probably of the 50s. No gilt. Goblet $150.00; wine $80.00. *Wine reproduced.*

No. 217 – RINGED FRAMED BLOCKS – Not previously listed. Similar to FRAMED BLOCKS, above, only this has the gilt trim, and additional fine rings above and below the heavy band. Clear flint either footed tumbler or spill shown. Very early, possibly the 40s. Footed tumbler or spill $80.00; goblet in this $150.00. *Recently, several have been found with too bright gold and no wear. Possibly reproductions.*

No. 205 – PANELLED FRAMES – Heretofore unlisted; as fine an example of early glass as I've ever seen. This one is in cold, electric blue flint. Unique, $150.00.

No. 165 – TERRACED BULL'S EYE – Mil – Pk. 2-150. This one is that opaque blue which we sometimes find in products of the Sandwich factory. Dr. Millard shows this in a dark green, with the early gilt flower trim. Base is hexagonal. Either the blue opaque or the green $250.00. Millard lists this of the 1880s which is, of course, wrong; it has all the ear marks of the 1850s and 1860s. *Transparent cobalt $350.00.*

No. 222 – OVAL PANELLED FRAMES – Heretofore unlisted. The line forming the bottom of the panel is lighter than those of the sides; pretty gilt trim in panels and dots above bars. Clear flint of the 1850s – 60s, octagonal base, this beauty belongs to Mr. Clarence Clawson. Goblet $150.00. *75% more for good decoration.*

No. 220 – FRAMED CIRCLES – Another of these previously unlisted very early, clear flint goblets. The similarity in pattern convinces one that they were probably made in the same or a close locale and possibly by workers who have designed for both factories. Goblet $150.00.

No. 208 – RINGED FRAMED OVALS – Another of the same list of hitherto unlisted clear flint goblets. Goblet $150.00.

ERRATA-EARLY AMERICAN PATTERN GLASS

Page 8 – No. 33 – Dutchess Loop – corrected and Pegged Flute put in after first printing.

Page 150 – No. 1701 – Minor Block – Mascotte has three rows. Same prices.

Page 32 – No. 308 – Bull's Eye and Rosette.

Page 202 – No. 2298 – Grand Inverted Thumbprint.

Page 202 – No. 2301 – Stanley Inverted Thumbprint.

Page 202 – No. 2304 – Tegman Inverted Thumbprint.

Page 202 – No. 2307 – Ohio Inverted Thumbprint.

Plus several patterns listed as American which were Canadian, of these I tell later in the book.

216
Horizontal Oval Frames

455
Elongated Thumbprint

65
Bull's Eye and Prism

64
Bull's Eye and
Broken Column—Page 9.
Footed Tumbler

145
Double Circles

22
Sawtooth with
Bull's Eye
Column

375
Ribbed Loop

35
Pillared Loop

No. 216 – HORIZONTAL OVAL FRAMES – Heretofore unlisted. Clear flint of the 50s; another of this early family as shown on preceding page. Goblet $150.00. *75% more in canary.*

No. 455 – ELONGATED THUMBPRINT – Note the difference between this and the later Almond Thumbprint. The thick stem and the two rows of deep elongated thumbprints shout its age as one of the earliest, possibly of the 40s. Goblet $150.00.

No. 65 – BULL'S EYE AND PRISM – On pl. 4 – Book 2, Dr. Millard shows this with a knob at the bottom of the stem. Clear flint of the late 50s or early 60s. Goblet $125.00.

No. 64 – BULL'S EYE AND BROKEN COLUMN – Mil. – Bk. 2-30. Clear flint of the early 60s. Slightly later than many of these. See page 8.

No. 145 – DOUBLE CIRCLES – Another very clear flint, differing slightly in design from the usual run. Probably of the 50s. Goblet $130.00.

No. 22 – SAWTOOTH WITH BULL'S EYE COLUMN – Flint of the late 50s or early 60s. On page of Lamps I show a lamp in the same pattern; this would again tend to indicate these early patterns were made in many pieces. How this old glass travels. I located one piece in Portland, Oregon, the other in Cape Cod, Massachusetts. Decanter $95.00.

No. 375 – RIBBED LOOP – Mil. – Bk. 2-149. Clear flint of the early 60s. Goblet $70.00.

No. 35 – PILLARED LOOP – Previously unlisted. I do not know whether the piece pictured was a spill or a spooner, but it is a choice piece of clear flint of the 50s. Spill or spooner $75.00. 100% more in canary.

Many of the fine old goblets on these pages came from the Nickerson collection or the collection of Dr. Bruce Swift in the Allen Art Museum at Oberlin, Ohio.

HOW TO COLLECT GLASS

Collect with a definite purpose, ask yourself these questions:

Do I want glass solely for decor, or for table service or for both?

Do I live formally or informally?

If for table service what kind of china do I have? What cloths? Can color of cloths be dyed?

Do I want pieces of old glass for gifts?

With a definite plan, decor, table usage, or gifts, set out to the most reliable dealer you can find, buy the best piece your pocketbook will allow. It is far better to save and buy one outstanding piece than several small, commonplace numbers. Remember, it is quality and not number that adds value to a collection.

Above all, don't collect without knowledge; don't expect dealers to teach you orally, your memory may be inaccurate anyhow, but you must read, re-read, and read again. Then too, you must try to see some of the things of which you read, elsewhere here I give a list of some of the fine choice spots to visit and even a way to lure non-collecting husbands to the collecting trail of study. I've done it.

84
Double Bull's Eye Plus

270
Divided Squares

107
Triple Bull's Eye Lamp

82
Triple Bull's Eye &
Loop Peg Lamp

379
Plain Miotin

178
Simplicity

No. 84 – DOUBLE BULL'S EYE PLUS – Heretofore unlisted. Flint sperm oil lamp of the 50s. I show these here as I'm confident there were other pieces in these patterns, and I hope to hear of them. Lamp $150.00.

No. 270 – DIVIDED SQUARES – Flint clear glass butter dish at the Sandwich Museum. I've never seen another piece of this, nor has it been listed, but certainly there was a set. This gives an idea of how much work there is still to be done in the pattern glass field. Butter dish, probably of the 60s. $125.00.

No. 107 – TRIPLE BULL'S EYE PLUS – Another unlisted, flint sperm oil lamp of the 40s. Clear glass $175.00.

No. 82 – TRIPLE BULL'S EYE AND LOOP PEG LAMP – The bowl of this lamp is small as it was for sperm oil as most peg lamps were. This has little value only as a specimen and type of lamp. Value $75.00. *A peg lamp has metal prongs on the "peg" to hold it tight in a candlestick.*

No. 379 – PLAIN MIOTIN – Mil.-4. A later, clear, non-flint goblet of the late 70s and early 80s put here because there was no room for it elsewhere. Also comes with red top. May possibly be found in flint. I'd like to hear. Non-flint clear $20.00; red top $30.00. A flint goblet in it would be worth $30.00.

No. 178 – SIMPLICITY – Heretofore unlisted. Clear flint of the 60s. Goblet $35.00. Should be a set.

CAN ONE EVER BE TOO CAREFUL?

A few years back, a magazine gave much fanfare to an article which it was about to publish, listing 100 fakes in old pattern glass. I was not too surprised when the article appeared, for I thought their writers were far from over paid. The writer was a fine, honest dealer, but one who did not have enough information to write such an article. When she heard I considered the writing most inaccurate, she wrote me and said it was not what she had written. I never knew; it carried her name. Patterns which have never been reproduced were listed as such, distinguishing marks which were all wrong were given. For instance a goblet in which there is no reproduction was so called because its measurements did not line up with the one at hand. A Pleat and Panel goblet was called new because the stippling was uneven, the truth is just the opposite – even stippling, new goblet; uneven stippling, old goblet, and so it went. I wondered for some time how some of this listing of fakes when they did not exist happened; then it came to me: In some of the earlier written glass books, the authors would list the glass as the first factory made it and then as another rival factory took it up, they would term it "a reproduction." As I've stated elsewhere many factories bought molds from firms which sold them and produced the same pattern, we do not term them "reproductions," as they are issued at, sometimes, the same time, sometimes, near the same territory. Then too, when the U.S. Glass Co. was formed from many small companies in the early 90s, many old molds were used and patterns of the 80s and possibly as far back as the 70s were around and reissued. These cannot be distinguished easily from the first issue and we do not try to. They are not reproductions. Glass molds are large and cumbersome and are not apt to be stored too long, although now and then, I run into a cache of old molds. I know of some which are stored and brought out occasionally to make reproductions for a comparatively small gift shop. Not too many are made and they are not marketed wholesale to any extent. It just goes to show that one can never be too positive in stating that there is no reproduction, especially in the non-flint and in the colors. Color is what is in demand and is what commands the price in non-flint so here is the danger zone.

90
Early Moon & Star

90
Early Moon & Star

90
Early Moon & Star

28
Reverse Colonial

Creamer

16
Block & Bar

Water Pitcher

126
Empire Colonial

127
Knob Stem Colonial

NO. 90 – EARLY MOON AND STAR – K. Bk. 8-P. 72 shows this and calls it OLD MOON AND STAR, but as that could be confused with a description of the much later, non-flint, unrelated pattern, I think this name better. I believe it to be of the 40s as the lamps shown in it are sperm oil and kerosene was invented in 1852. It is a brilliant flint made in clear, canary and probably other colors. Mr. Nicholson has some canary shards of a sugar bowl which were dug up at the site of the New England Glass Co. It is very scarce; very little of it has come to light. Covered sugar $150.00; creamer $125.00; spooner $85.00; lamps shown $175.00; *tumbler $100.00.*

No. 28 – REVERSE COLONIAL – Shown by Lowell Innes in his *Early Glass of the Pittsburgh District.* He says it is a sweetmeat dish made by McKee. Pittsburgh Glass is in heavy demand – the early Pittsburgh, that is: Sweetmeat dish shown $100.00. *Glass sometimes has gray color.*

No. 16 – BLOCK AND BAR – K. Bk. 5-p. 45 shows this pitcher and states it might not be American. It most definitely is. Clear flint of the 50s. I found the creamer in the Nickerson collection, and the water pitcher is in the Sandwich museum. Creamer $150.00; water pitcher $500.00.

No. 126 – EMPIRE COLONIAL – Mil. 7. Clear flint of the 40s. All of the ear marks of very early glass: simple design, short, thick stem. Goblet $100.00; sugar w/cover $175.00.

No. 127 – KNOB STEM COLONIAL – formerly unlisted colonial. This one is later than the one above. Clear flint of the early 60s. Goblet $80.00. This goblet is in the collection of Mr. Clarence Clawson.

HOW TO STUDY PATTERN GLASS
WHAT AND HOW TO READ

It's as important how you read as what you read. In the first place, you cannot expect one book to cover china, furniture, brass, and all kinds of glass and be halfway accurate. A book which is accurate must be read more than once to get its full import. I suppose one should glide through first to satisfy her curiosity, but that is not really reading. To do that, read a small section at a time, try to see some of the things about which you have read, if possible, read other standard texts. Always not last date of copyright and date of revisions. To say a book is revised means nothing, it may have been revised a year or two after it was written and the original author may not be here now. New information is constantly becoming uncovered and it means constant study to keep up.

When one goes to the library, he cannot expect to get expert guidance on reading in so technical a subject from librarians, most of whom can do nothing but judge by title. Many librarians have nothing on their shelves but the books put out by the large publishing firms and many of the specialist's books are privately published and these libraries are not aware of their existence. If you read some magazine on your subject, however, you are bound to find them, sooner or later. I can't imagine a person who wants to be informed, not reading some periodical. Elsewhere I've listed a suggested list of books.

Glassmakers refer to the actual molden and solid glasses as "metal" no matter leaded or limeglass.

Decanter

118 Ashburton with Sawtooth
Handled Whiskey

256
Diag.
Sawtooth Band

56
Cut Oval Panels

19
Pressed Block

11
Victoria Compote

14
Etched Oval Panels

No. 118 – ASHBURTON WITH SAWTOOTH – Not previously listed; stopper, of course, is later. Clear flint of the 50s. This piece belongs to Mr. Kingsley of Portland, Oregon, and the other piece I show was in the Sandwich Museum. Handled decanter $200.00.

No. 118 – ASHBURTON WITH SAWTOOTH HANDLED WHISKEY – This is the piece from the Sandwich Museum. Handled whiskey $125.00. Here we are – East coast – West coast!

No. 256 – DIAGONAL SAWTOOTH BAND – Listed in my Booklet 1. There is a goblet in this at the Sandwich Museum. Clear flint of the 50s. Wine $30.00; goblet $80.00. Very scarce.

No. 11 – VICTORIA COMPOTE – More of this pattern has appeared. Of the late 50s and early 60s, clear and colors, I know not which, only I know there is a covered canary Victoria sugar bowl in the Ford Museum. Tall 8" and 10" covered compote $150.00; 6" covered sweetmeat dish $100.00; covered butter $110.00; 9" cakestand $125.00; 15" cakestand $300.00. Open compotes worth only a fraction of covered ones; any size $50.00.

No. 19 – PRESSED BLOCK – Mil. Bk. 2-97. Clear flint of the 50s. Goblet $60.00.

No. 14 – ETCHED OVAL PANELS – Heretofore unlisted. From the collection of Mrs. Kenneth Wakefield. Goblet $65.00.

No. 56 – CUT OVAL PANELS – This one is in the collection of Mr. Clarence Clawson of Ohio. Clear flint of the 50s, very like the one next to it, Etched Oval Panels. Goblets $95.00.

HOW AM I TO JUDGE A DEALER?

You don't know glass, so you can't judge his stock. Here are some tips. Age does not improve some. It simply helps their ability to concoct yarns. If you see a stock loaded with all or many of the pitfall patterns listed here and a preponderance of colored rarities, beware. Most dealers in old glass have customers waiting for these things and they do not accumulate too many at a time.

Do not think because a dealer puts out an entire collection that it is fake. We are having to get most of our stock by buying collections at present; attics have been emptied. Do not be impressed by swank or saccharine compliments; good merchandise sells itself in normal business fashion.

Do not be impressed by either Sairey Gamp recommend or condemnation. Pay no attention to Mrs. Gusher who says, "Why don't you go to Jack's. His glass is so pretty and full of color." It probably is, fakes galore and the little pitcher he gives the nice lady as bait was a chipped fake.

Do not condemn a dealer because he made one mistake; give him a chance to right it; then watch and see if the faulty piece is returned to stock. If he tries to sell it again he was not sorry for his mistake.

If you do get a fake, insist on refund; remember every penny to the coffer of these people is a step in abetting all fakers.

327
Bulb Stem Sawtooth

331
Sawtooth Plain Stem

328
Umbilicated Sawtooth

68
Prism and Sawtooth

475
Prism and
Flattened Sawtooth

196
Sawtooth and
Block Thumbprint

428
Bennington Inverted
Thumbprint

478
Acme Inverted
Thumbprint

No. 327 – BULB STEM SAWTOOTH – Listed, but not pictured in my first book. This is one of the early forms of the pattern. I believe the creamers and covered pieces of this and the Knob stem variety are interchangeable. The prices for either pattern would be: sauce $9.50; spooner $25.00; goblet $50.00; covered salt $80.00; creamer $75.00; covered sugar $60.00; celery $50.00; open salt, plain edge $10.00; open sugar $15.00; covered butter $55.00; large cakestand $110.00; water pitcher $150.00. If you compare this with prices quoted for KNOB STEM SAWTOOTH in my first book you will see how the story of desirable flint glass is going. *Applied handle.*

No. 331 – SAWTOOTH – PLAIN STEM – BANDED – Mil. 26-L. 41 calls this SAWTOOTH OF THE LATER PERIOD. This is what it is, a clear non-flint of the 70s, made in many pieces. In this the goblet has the teeth ending in a plain band at the top, while there is another in LATER SAWTOOTH which has the teeth forming the pointed top band. Same vintage, same prices as LATER SAWTOOTH shown in my first book, Goblet $35.00.

No. 328 – UMBILICATED SAWTOOTH – Listed but not pictured in my first book. Same vintage and same values as BULB STEM SAWTOOTH above.

No. 68 – PRISM AND SAWTOOTH – Mil. Bk. 2-152. Clear flint of the 60s. So far, seen only in goblet $50.00.

No. 475 – PRISM AND FLATTENED SAWTOOTH – Mil. Bk. 2-19 – RIBBED PINEAPPLE – L.V. 23. Clear flint of the 50s or possibly the 60s for here is another pattern in which we find the small bowled lamp and matching spill. Goblet $75.00; spooner or spill $50.00; lamp $80.00.

No. 196 – SAWTOOTH AND BLOCKED THUMBPRINT – K. Bk. 8-8 calls it simply BLOCKED THUMBPRINT. Non-flint of the early 70s or 60s but from looks of creamer should be found in flint; the creamer having a beautiful applied handle and the shape of the early ones. Spooner or spill shown $40.00; open sugar $20.00; covered sugar $45.00; creamer $35.00. In flint it would be an additional 50%.

No. 428 – BENNINGTON INVERTED THUMBPRINT – Mil. – 169. Clear and much color of the late 70s and 80s, made in many colors. Clear goblet $20.00; clear wine $15.00; canary wine $30.00; canary goblet $40.00; amber wine $20.00; amber goblet $30.00; blue wine $30.00; blue goblet $40.00.

No. 478 – ACME INVERTED THUMBPRINT – Mil. Bk. 2-77 – Another clear and colored non-flint of the 70s and 80s. Values the same as for BENNINGTON THUMBPRINT. Profusely reproduced. If puzzled as to difference between these two thumbprints all one needs to remember is that the Acme has round print while in the Bennington they are angular.

43
Panelled Punty

163
Lined Long Panels

395
Brooklyn Flute

397
Pennsylvania Flute

135
Spiked Argus

383
Argosy

1414
Wahoo

231
Stymied Loops

No. 43 – PANELLED PUNTY – Clear flint of the 50s. Base of sugar shown. Goblet $195.00; wine $70.00; covered sugar $90.00; open sugar $30.00; creamer $200.00; *spill $95.00.* Rare.

No. 163 – LINED LONG PANELS – This was listed for the first time in my Booklet 6. Clear flint of the 50s. *Boston & Sandwich Co.* Tumbler $60.00; *mug $125.00; vase $100.00; cologne $125.00; Opaque or colors 200% more.*

No. 395 – BROOKLYN FLUTE – Listed but not pictured in my first book; goblet now $45.00.

No. 397 – PENNSYLVANIA FLUTE – Previously unlisted. This is unusual in that while patterned like the older flutes of the 50s and 60s, this pattern is non-flint, evidently of the late 70s or early 80s and is colored, a medium blue. In clear $20.00; in blue shown $50.00.

No. 135 – SPIKED ARGUS – Mil. Bk. 2-149. Clear flint of the mid 60s. Wine $30.00; goblet $75.00.

No. 383 – ARGOSY – Mil. – 162. Clear flint of the 60s. Goblet $50.00.

No. 1414 – WAHOO – Mil. – 39. I believe this goblet was made from the late 60s through the early 70s as it is found both in flint and non-flint. Non-flint goblet $20.00; flint goblet $50.00.

No. 231 – STYMIED LOOPS – Mil. Bk. 2-155. Flint of the late 1860s. Clear goblet $75.00.

103
Choked Ashburton

99
Giant Straight Stemmed
Ashburton

105
Slim Ashburton

94
Near Slim
Ashburton

111
Double Knob
Stem Ashburton

102
Proxy Ashburton

112
Short
Ashburton

109
Semi-Squared
Ashburton

ASHBURTON

Ashburton was made over a long period of time, from the 40s to the 70s, the later was non-flint and is unimportant as far as collectors are concerned. I show the different types of goblets which were made, so that people who order by mail and who advertise will know how to describe what they are talking about. The remainder of the sets are interchangeable. The Ashburton creamer, by its sheer beauty of line has made more than one convert to early American pattern glass. It is interesting to combine more than one kind of the goblet; from the pictures, one can judge the harmonizing types.

No. 103 – CHOKED ASHBURTON – Mil. – 5. One of the more commonly found ones. Of course, I'm considering only flint ones here. Goblet $50.00.

No. 99 – GIANT STRAIGHT STEMMED ASHBURTON – Mil. 5 shows this with knob at bottom of stem, but this is first listing of it with plain stem. A decidedly wide bowl, goblet $55.00.

No. 105 – SLIM ASHBURTON – Mil. 6. A nicely proportioned one. Goblet $45.00.

No. 94 – NEAR SLIM ASHBURTON – Heretofore unlisted. Very close to No. 105, only in this the ovals are connected and are stretched slightly wider. Goblet $45.00.

No. 111 – DOUBLE KNOB STEM ASHBURTON – Previously unlisted, a very scarce type with two knobs on the stem. Goblet $50.00.

No. 102 – PROXY ASHBURTON – Mil. 5. Another well-known form. Goblet $45.00.

No. 112 – SHORT ASHBURTON – Mil. Bk. 2-142. Another one of the scarcer type but not well known; would combine well with Squared and Semi-Squared. Goblet $45.00.

No. 109 – SEMI-SQUARED ASHBURTON – Heretofore unlisted; very like 112, only in 112 the panels meet while in this, they are separated by a thin strip. Goblet $45.00.

NOTE: The other pieces of the sets are interchangeable. Wine $40.00; Champagne, claret, 5¾", cordial $80.00; bitters bottle $60.00; decanter, no stopper $150.00; with pewter stopper $190.00; with original glass stopper $225.00; single egg cup $40.00; double egg cup $80.00; honey dish or flat sauce $10.00; rare handled large tumbler $125.00; regular tumbler $80.00; whiskey tumbler $75.00; water bottle with tumble up $95.00; very rare covered Toddy jar and plate $300.00; *celery $150.00. Color rare and 300% more+.*

Ashburton was reproduced in colors in the 1960s to 1970s in non-flint. Forms not identical.

96
Talisman
Ashburton

101
Barrel Ashburton

108
Flaring Top Ashburton

111
Ashburton Celery

100
Differing
Ashburton

161
Creased Worchester

159
Straight Banded
Worchester

410
Stepped Flute

No. 96 – TALISMAN ASHBURTON – Mil. – 5. Very like BARREL ASHBURTON and these two and SLIM combine very nicely. Goblet $45.00.

No. 101 – BARREL ASHBURTON – Shown in my first book, but I'm repeating it here, so I can show the difference between it and TALISMAN, above. In the latter, there is a small strip between the top ovals while in TALISMAN they touch, then too, the latter has a slightly heavier stem. Goblet $45.00.

No. 108 – FLARING TOP ASHBURTON – Heretofore unlisted, quite unusual, heavier than some, with elongated panels and altogether quite different. Goblet $45.00.

No. 111 – ASHBURTON CELERY – There are at least two types of celeries, one with plain top, and one with scalloped top. One shown $100.00; scalloped top $150.00; canary yellow, extremely rare $1200.00; *green $1200.00.*

No. 100 – DIFFERING ASHBURTON – Hitherto unlisted. The only one of the well-known family which I've seen which has a knob at the top of the stem. Its thick, short stem, plus its scarcity proclaims it an early member of the family. Goblet $45.00.

No. 161 – CREASED WORCHESTER – Mil. – 12. Knob stem, clear flint of the 50s or early 60s. Wine $45.00; egg cup $35.00; goblet $45.00.

No. 159 – STRAIGHT BANDED WORCHESTER – Mil. 6. Clear flint of early 60s. Note that in this pattern the design is made by putting loops opposite one another instead of staggering them as in ASHBURTON. Fairly common; goblet $45.00; *tumbler $45.00. Canary, green, or blue 200% more. Boston & Sandwich Glass Co.*

No. 410 – STEPPED FLUTE – Clear flint of the 40s. This is another pattern which Mrs. Kamm thought might be foreign and she shows the creamer under another name. I believe it is definitely American; I thought that when I found the goblet and then when I found the covered sugar which shrieked of an American manufacture. Goblet $65.00; creamer $95.00; covered sugar $110.00.

120
Excelsior with Maltese Cross

113
Barrel Excelsior

154
Excelsior Plus

121
Tong

514
Fine Prism

29
Collared Bull's Eye

44
Dia. Filled Ovals

46
Diamond in Ovals

No. 120 – EXCELSIOR WITH MALTESE CROSS – Mi. – 162. Clear flint of the 50s. Note that this has a definite Maltese cross and it also has a double knob stem. Wine, egg cup $45.00; goblet $60.00; creamer $75.00; covered sugar $90.00.

No. 113 – BARREL EXCELSIOR – Listed and pictured in my first book; footed tumbler shown for comparison with EXCELSIOR PLUS below.

No. 154 – EXCELSIOR PLUS – Heretofore unlisted. This is almost the same as the one above. Only here, a small diamond protrudes between the ovals, instead of being indented, and there is an additional row of scallops around the base. Of the same vintage and same values as BARREL EXCELSIOR. The prices of the following should now be raised to: cordials $90.00; wines, champagnes $80.00; egg cups $30.00; tumblers $45.00; footed tumblers $80.00; goblets $75.00.

No. 121 – TONG – K. Bk. 5-24, L. V. 25, calls it EXCELSIOR VARIANT, but of course, I do not believe in the term "variant" because we do not know which pattern was the original and which one followed. Clear flint of the 50s *and 60s.* Spooner or spill $50.00; celery, shown $75.00; tall open compote $45.00; covered compote $150.00; covered sugar $95.00; creamer $110.00. No goblet has ever come to light; there should be one. *Grayed glass worth 25% less.*

No. 514 – PRISM – Goblet pictured and listed in my book. This is the whiskey taster; scarcely 2" in height. Whiskey taster $35.00; I show it here to prove that this was also made in sets. This is one of the many lining the kitchen of Mrs. Kenneth Wakefield on the Cape in Mass.

There is some debate over "whiskey tasters." It is very likely they were toy glasses. Sandwich made a great deal of toy or miniature glass from their earliest days.

No. 29 – COLLARED BULL'S EYE – A very heavy, early (the 40s) piece of clear flint glass. Heretofore unlisted. I think there was more of this pattern. Information, please. Salt shown $35.00. *Many salts were individual patterns, other forms not found.*

No. 44 – DIAMOND FILLED OVALS – Previously unlisted, bell toned tumbler of the late 50s. Listed and shown in my Booklet 6. Tumbler $75.00.

No. 46 – DIAMONDS IN OVALS – Mil. Bk. 2-65. Clear flint of the 60s. Resembles closely one above only this is not quite as heavy glass and has the small row of diamonds added below. Goblet $95.00.

412
Pittsburgh Flute

409
Elegant

411
Dutchess Loop Ale

404
Spatula

371
Loop and Crystal

374
Knob Stem
Loop & Crystal

378
Semi-Loops

411
Dutchess Loop

No. 412 – PITTSBURGH FLUTE – Listed, but not pictured, in my first book. Goblet now $35.00.

No. 409 – ELEGANT – Mil. Bk. 2-4. clear flint of the early 60s. Goblet $35.00.

No. 411 – DUTCHESS LOOP – In the first printing of my book, this was put in for a Pegged Flute picture. We caught the error after the first printing. Goblet now $35.00.

No. 404 – SPATULA – Mil. Bk. 2-155. Clear flint of the early 60s. Goblet $35.00.

No. 371 – LOOP AND CRYSTAL – Mil. Bk. 2-111. Clear flint of the 60s. Goblet is a shape not frequently found in this period $70.00; *mug with applied handle $100.00. McKee & Bros. 1864.*

No. 374 – KNOB STEM LOOP AND CRYSTAL – Mil. Bk. 2-151. This certainly in no way resembles the goblet next to it, to which Dr. Millard gives the same family name. However, I feel so strongly that all of this changing of names causes so much confusion that I shall leave it, as my purpose is standardization of names. Goblets $45.00.

No. 378 – SEMI-LOOPS – Not heretofore listed. Clear flint of the early 60s. Goblet $35.00.

No. 411 – DUTCHESS LOOP ALE – Ale in pattern shown above, value $45.00.

WHEN IS AN IMPERFECTION, A PERFECTION? A DEFECT?

Collecting old glass is primarily an exercise of using judgment. Just when is a flaw bad enough to become a defect? It's really a question of degree in some cases. If one is looking for mechanical perfection, go to the modern; the Creator in making His most beautiful work, never made any two exactly the same — there is no other human being in which both sides are identical. The human eye is a delicate machine which wearies quickly and dislikes monotony also. This accounts for our liking handmade articles and articles which have not become so mass produced and so machine perfected that they have lost the human touch. But if a thing is too crooked it becomes crippled as do noticeable chips and cracks and they offend our sensibilities. A so-called "straw" line is not a straw line but is caused by cooling and is not a defect unless again it is so marked that it assumes the appearance of a blemish. I do not believe our thrifty ancestors threw away every dish with a slight chip, especially if it were where it did not show or did not harm its use. A chip on a drinking rim is out, of course. At times, in those days, when processes were not controlled by the electric eye and other mechanical gadgets, too much glass would be in the mold; as the glass was removed a rough spot might result at the mold joining mark at the base. This is not a defect. All defects should be listed on dealers' listings wherever they occur and prices should be made accordingly. Stained glass is definitely defective. I think it only fair to list whether a glass is clear, stained, greyed or "sick glass"; or tinted amethyst. The latter may be caused by original formula or by being exposed to direct bright sunlight over a long period of time. "Sick glass" is this glass which appears greasy and has lost its sheen. This can be caused by storing glass wrapped in paper in a cold, damp place for long period of time. I know of no cure for any glass ailments and I do not believe in grinding edges; there are dealers who do; you can spot a ground edge; there are those who take a clear pattern and do the acid etching. I like none of these tricks.

Please remember, mechanical perfection is sterile; the Master Hand did not use it, possibly to encourage us in our attempts at perfection. The attempt is all right, but remember common sense and its warning: "We're only humans."

*Ground rims will be flat and sharp edged, factory finish will be rounder.

338
Crystal Trimmed

339
Pointed Stem Crystal

337
Banded Crystal-Knob
Stem

340
Banded Crystal-Balb
Stem

343
Slim Crystal

338
Crystal-Knob Stem Creamer

1933
Crystal with Honeycomb Creamer

400
Connecticut Flute

No. 338 – CRYSTAL* – L.-2 and 11. Clear flint of the 60s. The crystal pattern I showed in my first book should have been named PLAIN STEM CRYSTAL (No. 340). I list the numerous pieces and prices in that book but prices on all flint have risen so now that a goblet is worth $25.00; a creamer $50.00; a covered sugar $60.00; an egg cup $20.00; celery $50.00. These prices are for flint. This pattern is easily confused with Huber which is really much heavier, especially in the stem and the stem is a trifle shorter. *Handled tumbler $60.00; handled egg cup $75.00.*

No. 337 – BANDED CRYSTAL – KNOB STEM – Heretofore unlisted. This one has knob at mid stem; early flint family as above; goblet $25.00; etched trim shown; also not etched.

No. 340 – BANDED CRYSTAL – As above with bulb stem and early type of gilt trim. Goblet $150.00. From the Sandwich Museum.

No. 339 – CRYSTAL-POINTED STEM – Note points where stem joins base. Clear flint of the 60s. Goblet $25.00.

No. 337 – KNOB STEM CRYSTAL CREAMER – Creamer of 337 above with gilt trim $45.00; covered sugar $65.00.

No. 343 – SLIM CRYSTAL – Hitherto unlisted form of this well known pattern; lighter, clear flint of the 60s, goblet $25.00.

No. 1933 – CRYSTAL WITH HONEYCOMB – Mil. Bk. 2-138. Non-flint of the late 70s or early 80s. In the goblet the pattern goes nearer to the edge. In the picture the dark spaces in the lower part are rows of Honeycomb. This is a late pattern, shown here for contrast with the early Crystal. Goblet in clear $15.00; in blue $40.00; creamer in clear $15.00; in blue $40.00.

No. 400 – CONNECTICUT FLUTE – Mil. 78. This, as many of the Flutes, was made over a long period of years, so we find it in flint and in lime glass. Listed but not pictured, in my first book. Clear flint goblet $45.00; blue, as one pictured $100.00.

Metz causes some confusion over what is "Crystal" and what is "Huber." Both are shown in McKee and Bros. 1868 catalog with no obvious difference between the two. "Huber" tends to be the more common usage today.

334
Huber-Pointed Stem

336
Flaring Huber

156
Flaring Grooved Bigler

559
Icicle and Loops

527
Triangular Prism

435
New York Honeycomb Covered Relish

525
Panelled Prisms

No. 334 – HUBER-POINTED STEM – Very like one shown in my first book, only in this, where with stem joins the base there are decided points. Goblets now $25.00.

No. 336 – FLARING HUBER – Mil. 21. This has stem decidedly pointed at the top and is quite a bit wider across the bowl of the goblet. Clear flint of the late 50s. Goblet $25.00. I believe the set pieces as in Ashburton, Flute, etc., are interchangeable; the prices on these would be those of the Pointed Huber above.

No. 156 – FLARING GROOVED BIGLER – Hitherto unlisted. Clear flint of the 50s. In this the panels are more rounded and the knobs on the stems are much more angular, then, too, this goblet has a very decided flared top. I've now seen other pieces in Bigler; prices apply to all types; goblet shown $75.00; wine $60.00; spoonholder or spill $45.00; footed tumbler $50.00; celery $110.00; covered sugar $110.00; creamer $90.00; *handled tumbler $125.00. Boston & Sandwich Glass Co.*

No. 559 – *BLAZE* – Mil. Bk. 2-137. Clear flint of the 60s; goblet has long thin stem. Egg cup, shown $60.00; goblet $95.00; spooner $40.00; covered sugar $75.00; creamer $65.00. *New England Glass Co.*

No. 435 – NEW YORK HONEYCOMB RELISH – I listed this in my first book but then I had not seen the covered dishes in it which are most attractive. Clear, non-flint of the early 70s. They would make a beautiful inexpensive setting to collect and very practical as this would make a fine modern butter dish and the covered sugar is not too large to be practical and non-flint Honeycomb wines and goblets are some of the easiest of this vintage to get. Wine $20.00; goblet $25.00; footed tumbler $30.00; egg cup $20.00; covered relish (shown) $50.00; covered butter $65.00; covered sugar $50.00. *50% more for flint.*

No. 527 – TRIANGULAR PRISM – Mil. Bk. 2-29. Clear flint of the 50s. I've found this in regular and ladies' size goblet but no other piece yet. Either goblet $65.00; *mug $50.00. Boston & Sandwich Glass Co.*

No. 525 – PANELS AND PRISMS – Heretofore unlisted. Clear flint of the 60s. All I've seen is goblet, $60.00.

2612
French Drape

234
Prism and Ball Compote

512
Flat Rib and Shell

496
Dickinson

443
Vaulted Smocking

91
Long Star

91
Long Star

No. 2612 – FRENCH DRAPE – This French goblet is shown here so it will not be confused with the American. It is clear flint. Note how fancy it is, trimming on every space where it could possibly be put, while the American of this era, the 60s, is very simple. Goblet $75.00. It is wise to have one or two foreign goblets in a collection as a basis of comparison and to give contrast.

No. 234 – PRISM AND BALL – Heretofore unlisted, clear flint of the 60s. I've seen two pieces, this, the 7" covered compote and the flat sauce. Flat sauce $5.00; covered compote $45.00; open compote $25.00. There undoubtedly was a setting. *Glass tends to be gray in color.*

No. 512 – FLAT RIB AND SHELL – Another previously unlisted clear flint of the 50s. The celery which I found in Maine is the only piece I've ever seen, but there surely was a set. Celery $125.00.

No. 496 – DICKINSON – L. V. 23 – Mil. 12. Clear flint of the 60s, made at the Sandwich factory. Flat sauce $9.00; spooner $40.00; open sugar $30.00; covered sugar $75.00; covered butter $85.00; creamer $50.00; open compote $30.00; covered compote $125.00; goblet $70.00; water pitcher $150.00; wine $45.00. Shown in my Booklet 2.

No. 443 – VAULTED SMOCKING – Listed for the first time in my Booklet 2. It and the creamer are in the Sandwich Museum and it is found in that vicinity. Clear flint of the 60s. Sugar never had a cover, $30.00; creamer $45.00.

No. 91 – LONG STAR – Listed in my Booklet 2 for the first time. A pair of these are in the Sandwich Museum, also. Clear flint of the 60s. Sugar never had a cover $30.00; creamer $45.00. All I've ever heard of are these two pieces.

MOLD MARKS

Before her death, Mrs. Ruth Webb Lee stressed the unimportance of mold marks. I've tried in everything I've written to make the point but people pay no heed, still lengthy descriptions pour in, mentioning first the number of mold marks. The number of mold marks has no significance whatsoever as regards age, value or anything else. Disregard them. The confusion possibly arose from a description of another ware, "three mold blown," which is not pattern glass and is not my field, and is not anything for pattern glass people to worry about. When you start to talk of mold marks you stamp yourself as a rank novice and one who never reads.

Note. The absence of mold marks on the bowls of pieces (goblets, wines, compotes, etc.) is the result of "fire polishing." After removal from the mold, the item would briefly be put back into the furnace until the mold lines melted and were obliterated.

457
Frosted Thumbprint

268
Fine Rib
with Cut Ovals
Two Rows

268
Fine Rib
with Cut Ovals
Two Rows

263
Fine Rib
with Cut Ovals
Three Rows

148
Panelled Triumphant

123
Tall Argus-Bulb stem

451
Argus—Five Rows

460
Giant Baby Thumbprint

No. 457 – FROSTED THUMBPRINT – First listed in my Booklet 3. Rare, beautiful flint, possibly of the early 40s as it has the thick stem; and the frosting may have been their way of making a not too brilliant glass have an attractive surface. That was what was done in the Lacy glass; all of these tiny angled surfaces reflected light and gave a sheen which they were not able to accomplish in the earliest days of the pressing machine. I've never heard of anything but the goblet in this pattern although there probably was more. Shards of it were found at the Sandwich factory site. Clear and frosted flint only. $175.00.

No. 268 – FINE RIB WITH TWO ROW CUT OVALS – Listed by me in my first book but at that time I had not seen the two row variety, nor had I seen as many pieces. Very fine, brilliant flint. Covered sugar $250.00; creamer $295.00; celery $175.00; goblet $400.00.

No. 263 – FINE RIB WITH CUT OVALS – THREE ROWS – Same age of the 50s, goblet $400.00.

No. 148 – PANELLED THUMBPRINT – Mil. 39. This goblet is really heavier than one would judge from its photo: it's a clear flint of the 60s which has not appeared in anything save the goblet. Goblet $60.00; if found in non-flint, that version would be worth only $30.00.

No. 123 – TALL ARGUS – BULB STEM – Mil. 2-28. In Bk. 1-3 Millard lists another Tall Argus which has an entirely different pattern. This is a beautiful, clear flint of the 50s. A scarce goblet $90.00.

No. 451 – ARGUS·– FIVE ROWS – Mil. Bk. 2-29. Clear flint of the 50s, another scarce one and another in which we've found nothing but the goblet. Goblet $75.00.

No. 460 – GIANT BABY THUMBPRINT – Mil. Bk. 2-40. Really no relative of the well-known Baby Thumbprint (Dakota) family, but a fine old flint of the 60s. Goblet $75.00. *Heavily reproduced in colored non-flint.*

STANDARDIZATION OF SIZES

I'm asked, How can one distinguish between a large wine and a champagne, a small goblet and a lady's goblet, a wine and cordial, is there a definite standard or rule. No, there is no definite set standard or rule, there is nothing one can do but learn what was made in the different patterns and what they were called. For instance, the Cordial in Hand is almost as large as most wines, Ashburton has about six sizes in goblets, none of which are lady's. It's most distressing, but I don't think there is anything one can do. Also, the difference between a claret and an ale is extremely finely drawn. I believe clarets are taller and possibly more slender.

There is just one point to remember in size, "Don't be a size crank." Don't insist all of your goblets be of exactly the same height, one fourth inch difference will never show at the distance they are on the table and dealers lose patience with fussy customers. We enjoy slight irregularities in old glass.

133
Round Thumbprint—
Lined Band Wine
Footed Tumbler

133

132
Round Thumbprints

141
Barrel Argus

147
Stocky Mirror

58
Prism and Lobular Loops

195
Prism and Bull's Eye
Column

12
Giant Sawtooth Tumbler

NO. 133 – LINED BAND – ROUND THUMBPRINT – Heretofore unlisted clear flint of the 60s. The thumbprints in footed tumbler shown here are as round as those in the wine also shown, the difference in appearance is due to the angle in which the picture was taken. Wine $35.00; footed tumbler $30.00; goblet $45.00.

No. 132 – ROUND THUMBPRINT – Heretofore unlisted, clear flint of the 60s, a close relative of No. 133 above, only in the latter there are the two concentric lines running around at the top of the thumbprints and these run higher on the bowl. Goblet $35.00.

No. 141 – BARREL ARGUS – Mil. 153. Clear heavy flint of the 40s. Note thick, short, heavy stem of the very early goblet. Goblet $50.00. The difference between this and Mirror is that in the latter the prints are round, while in this, they are horizontal oval.

No. 147 – STOCKY MIRROR – Previously unlisted – Stem much shorter and thicker than in Mirror Mil. 1 or the one listed by me in my first book. I believe this to be the earliest form, of the 40s. Clear flint. Goblet $50.00.

No. 58 – PRISM AND LOBULAR PRINTS – Heretofore unlisted. Clear flint of the 40s with the usual ear marks of the time: short, thick stem. As in the case of many of these, only the goblet has come to light so far. I'd be so happy to hear of other pieces, especially creamer, sugar, etc. Goblet $70.00. *Commonly found in Great Britain.*

No. 195 – PRISM AND BULL'S EYE COLUMN – Heretofore unlisted. Clear flint of the 50s. Goblet $85.00.

No. 12 – GIANT SAWTOOTH – Clear, somewhat crude flint of the late 30s which I show in my first book. I'm showing the tumbler here because some don't recognize it as the tumbler to the pattern. The heavy teeth form little feet. Tumbler $50.00; spill $75.00; goblet now $125.00; whale oil lamp $200.00.

445
Early Thumbprint

445
Early Thumbprint

449
Hotel Argus

448
Hotel Thumbprint

169
Knob Stem Mirror

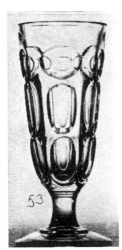

53
Round and
Oval Prints

171
Bulb Stem Mirror

52
Long Petal and
Thumbprint

No. 445 – EARLY THUMBPRINT – Mil-154 calls it GIANT BABY THUMBPRINT. Lee 59, 15, 18 shows pages from old Bakewell Pears catalogue (Pittsburgh) proving that they are at least one of the firms who made the pattern. It is no relative of the Baby Thumbprint pattern, but a clear flint of the 60s, made in many forms. Shown in my Booklet 3; honey and sauce dish $7.50; footed salt $35.00; flat relish dish $15.00; egg cup $30.00; spooner $30.00; jelly dish $35.00; wine glass $55.00; water tumbler $35.00; footed tumbler $35.00; cordial $55.00; handled beer mug $100.00; small open compote $45.00; open sugar $30.00; covered sugar $70.00; creamer $60.00; tall cakestand $150.00; celery $65.00; covered compote 4" $75.00; 8", 10" 125.00; rare 13½" covered compote $500.00; punch bole 12½" tall x 13½" diameter $800.00; water bottle with "tumble up" $125.00; castor bottle $30.00; 8" plate $60.00; syrup jug $200.00. Many of these pieces vary in style as do the goblets. Goblets pictured here is most desirable type. *Covered compotes have spherical shape.*

No. 445– EARLY THUMBPRINT – Footed tumbler to pattern shown. Same as above.

No. 449 – HOTEL ARGUS – L.24. Clear, made over a long period of time from the 60s through the 70s, therefore found in flint and non-flint, by Bakewell Pears and many other firms; goblet, non-flint $20.00; flint $35.00.

No. 448 – HOTEL THUMBPRINT – Mil.-1. Clear flint of the 60s. This was probably made in non-flint also. Flint goblet $35.00; non-flint goblet $20.00.

No. 169 – KNOB STEM MIRROR – Clear flint of the 60s. Ale shown. Heretofore unlisted. Note this has sharp knob at base of stem, ale, goblet $55.00.

No. 171 – BULB STEM MIRROR – Clear flint of the 60s. Ale shown. Previously unlisted; goblet, ale $55.00.

No. 53 – ROUND AND OVAL PRINTS – Clear flint of the 60s. Another one that has not been shown before. Ale, goblet $50.00.

No. 52 – LONG PETAL AND THUMBPRINT – Clear flint of the early 50s; goblet $60.00; ale $70.00. These four ales shown above are from the collection of Mr. Nickerson whose home is close to the Sandwich and the New England Glass Co. sites. He is a real student of old glass and his collection is a joy to see. I feel I have not given credit to him for all of the pieces of his which are pictured here but my enthusiasm for the glass prevented accurate record keeping. How mistaken some folks are who feel they have exhausted the study of Pattern Glass and who leave for greener fields; the hunt is getting more exciting every year. One does not have to resort to trash, we know little of much of the fine early glass and real students are needed in the field.

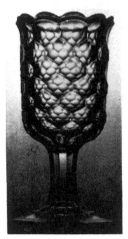

88
Vernon Honeycomb
Celery

425
Four Row Honeycomb

434
Honeycomb with
Diamond

421
Looped Band
Honeycomb

422
Loop with Honeycomb
Band

431
Honeycomb Band

439
Honeycomb with Pillar

433
Stretched Honeycomb

No. 88 – VERNON HONEYCOMB – Clear flint of the 50s. Made by the New England Glass Co. and probably others. The Honeycomb pattern has always been a way of dividing space, and these patterns will show you a few of the combinations of its uses, thousands of ways of splitting space into interesting units of design. The celery shown is a beauty, thick stem, clear flint glass, bell tones, with every mark of early manufacture. Price for celery of this quality would be $65.00; blue, scarce $200.00; *pitcher $150.00; spooner $45.00; compote, covered $175.00.*

No. 425 – FOUR ROW HONEYCOMB – Previously unlisted until shown in my Booklet 3. Clear non-flint of the 80s when countless numbers of this type were made for the eating places. It is not essential that a table setting match exactly and these non-flint Honeycombs furnish an inexpensive set of old glass to harmonize with early Americana. Goblet $30.00; and can frequently be found for less.

No. 434 – HONEYCOMB WITH DIAMOND – Mil. 96. Note definite small diamonds between honeycombs. Clear flint of the 60s, rayed base. Goblet all that has been found so far. Goblet $35.00.

No. 421 – LOOPED BAND HONEYCOMB – Mil.-10. Clear, non-flint of the 70s – 80s. Only goblet now $25.00.

No. 422 – LOOP WITH HONEYCOMB BAND – Mil. Bk. 2-64. Clear, non-flint of the 70s. Goblet $25.00.

No. 431 – HONEYCOMB BAND – Mil. 10. Clear goblet of the late 60s and early 70s. Has been seen only in flint $35.00; non-flint would be $20.00.

No. 439 – HONEYCOMB WITH PILLAR – Mil. Bk. 2-44. Non-flint of the early 80s; found in clear only. Goblet $30.00.

No. 433 – STRETCHED HONEYCOMB – Previously unlisted, clear, non-flint of the 70s; only goblet found. Goblet, non-flint $30.00; if found in flint $20.00. I hope to hear of other pieces in these and in flints of those listed as non-flint.

WHAT GLASS KNOWLEDGE IS IMPORTANT?

The knowledge of quality and a sense of fitness of the usage I'd say was our most important knowledge in the field of glass. Exact data as to locale and time of manufacture cannot be accurately given. Original trade names frequently do nothing but confuse, but knowing quality, that is what is good design and material, what is flint or lead glass and what is line and the approximate time of each — that is vital. To have working knowledge of fakes and shady business practices is also good. Real knowledge gives depth; walking encyclopedias never go far; they are not "nice to be near to."

Note: Allover honeycomb is generally called Vernon and partial covered bowl is New York Honeycomb. Many variations since nearly all glass companies made some form of "honeycomb."

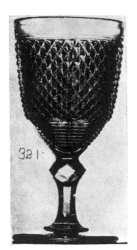

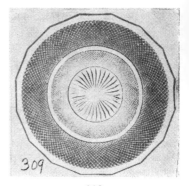

321
Diamond Point with
Ribs

325
Diamond Point with
Flutes

309
Fine Diamond Point

309
Fine Diamond Point

319
Diamond Point
Fancy Knob Stem

1699
Dia. Point Band

2157
Dewdrop

1913
English Hobnail—
Printed

No. 321 – DIAMOND POINT WITH RIBS – Mil. Bk. 2-2. Listed but not pictured in my first book. This is very much like Diamond Point, 334, shown there, only this has the concentric ribs at the base of the bowl. Its value would be the same as that of the other Diamond Point shown there with the exception of the goblet which would be $70.00; prices on 320 now would be flat sauce $7.50; spooner $40.00; open sugar $30.00; footed salt $25.00; jelly glass $30.00; egg cup $35.00; wine $35.00; whiskey tumbler, footed tumbler $40.00; many sizes open bowls $15.00 – 40.00; covered bowls $50.00; covered sugar $75.00; creamer $75.00; celery $45.00; open compotes $45.00; water bottle with tumble up $125.00; complete castor set $200.00.

No. 325 – DIAMOND POINT WITH FLUTES – Mil. Bk. 2-64. Another of the flint Diamond Point family; all clear flint of the 60s. This goblet $70.00. Other pieces as above. In the Sandwich Museum I saw a piece in Diamond Point that was hard to believe, a covered egg cup in opalescent canary is about the nearest to the description I can give of the color. Pieces like this are unique and can command any price.

No. 309 – FINE DIAMOND POINT – The points on this are finer like those on the plate which has been listed before but this type of goblet has never been noted previously. There's something about the etching that makes me think of the New England Glass Co. Goblet $55.00.

No. 309 – FINE DIAMOND POINT PLATE – L.-44 shows this plate but calls it DIAMOND POINT, the same as the much coarser pattern on 45, only one shown on the plate 45 has a star center. Plate shown, brilliant bell toned flint, value $45.00, size 7" diameter, of the 50s.

No. 319 – DIAMOND POINT – FANCY KNOB STEM – Clear, non-flint of the 80s. Goblet $40.00.

No. 1699 – DIAMOND POINT BAND – Mil. Bk. 2-33. Clear, non-flint of the 80s, which comes, at times with a gilt or red top; this flashy fellow is really not a member of the old Diamond Point family. Shown in my Booklet 6; goblet, wine $30.00; with red top $45.00; *pitcher $60.00; tumbler $35.00; mug $30.00; ruby stain 100% more; green stain 80% more.*

No. 2157 – DEWDROP WITH DIAMOND QUILTED TOP – Mil. Bk. 2-36. Clear and non-flint of the 70s. To date only goblet noted. Goblet, clear $20.00; canary $40.00; amber $25.00; blue $35.00.

No. 1913 – ENGLISH HOBNAIL – PRINTED – Mil.-91. Clear, non-flint of the 80s. Goblet $20.00. Probably are other pieces.

550
Icicle with
Chain Band

549
Icicle with Bulb Stem

510
Prism—Rayed Based

518
Pannelled Finetooth

261
Flute with Pleat Band

271
Flute with Fine Pleat

259
Prism Band

246
Hamilton with Frosted
Leaf

NO. 550 – ICICLE WITH CHAIN BAND – Listed but not pictured in my first book. Clear flint of the 60s. Wine now $60.00.

No. 549 – ICICLE WITH BULB STEM – Listed but not pictured in my first book Clear flint of the 60s. Mil. Bk. 2-42; Millard errs in putting these flints in the 70s as the flints were made prior to the Civil War for that disaster used the lead for bullets and hastened the finding of the lime glass formula. Non-flint wine $15.00; goblet $25.00; flint wine $45.00; goblet $55.00.

No. 510 – PRISM-RAYED BASE – Mil. 75 – L.-13. Clear flint of the late 50s found in several forms; wine $35.00; goblet $55.00; footed tumbler $35.00; creamer $500.00; decanter $75.00; covered sugar $60.00; water pitcher $150.00.

No. 518 – PANELLED FINETOOTH – Mil. Bk. 2-28. Clear flint of the 60s. Only goblet seen so far. Goblet $50.00.

No. 261 – FLUTE WITH PLEAT BAND – Mil. Bk. 2-105. Clear, non-flint of the 80s. May possibly be found in flint. Non-flint goblets $20.00. Flint would be worth $40.00.

No. 271 – FLUTE WITH FINE PLEAT BAND – Previously unlisted. Clear flint of the 60s. When I found this one, I felt quite sure that some time I would find 261, above, in flint, too, they seem so much alike. Flint goblet $40.00.

No. 259 – PRISM BAND* – Unlisted until shown in my Booklet No. 1. Clear flint of the mid 60s. Wine shown $25.00; goblet $35.00.

No. 246 – HAMILTON WITH FROSTED LEAF – Listed but not pictured, in my first book. Clear and frosted flint of the 50s made in many forms, becoming quite scarce due to heavy demand. Flat sauce, honey dish $20.00; spooner $45.00; open sugar $35.00; footed salt $50.00; egg cup $60.00; tumbler $100.00; wine $100.00; goblet $150.00; creamer with applied handle $150.00; with molded handle $60.00; covered sugar $90.00; celery $95.00; mug with applied handle $300.00; low open compote $60.00; tall open compote $80.00; low covered compote $100.00; tall covered compote $150.00; rare tumbler mold made hat $200.00; lamp $200.00. *30% less for no frosting. Made by Cape Cod Glass Co. Frosting was accomplished by grinding on an abrasive wheel, so it is rather rough to the touch. The later process of using acid produces a more satiny finish.*

* There is a look alike wine in non-flint of poorer quality known as Cartridge Belt value $6.00.

315
Four Petal

469
Disced Prism

470
Double Disced Prism

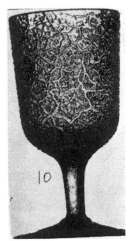

10
Sandwich Overshot

180
Stepped Hexagons

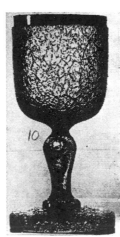

10
Sandwich Overshot
Gilt Trim

184
Ray

93
Tiny Long Star

No. 315 – FOUR PETAL – Flint, clear, of the early 60s. Listed but not pictured in my first book. Domed or pagoda type covered sugar shown; this one $150.00 with plain cover $135.00. The creamer which is not quite as bulbous has of course, an applied handle and is large $110.00. At present these are the only pieces that have come to light but surely there must have been others. *Reproduced sugar marked for Henry Ford Museum in flint.*

No. 469 – DISCED PRISM – Heretofore unlisted, clear flint of the 50s. Goblet $60.00.

No. 470 – DOUBLE DISCED PRISM – Previously unlisted, clear flint of the 50s. Goblet has usually thick stem, found in so many of the very early ones. Goblet $110.00.

No. 10 – *TREE OF LIFE* (SANDWICH) – Another of the Overshot goblets. This one having the gilt trim so frequently found on Overshot. Same value $60.00. This one is in the Sandwich Museum. *The goblet pictured is not "overshot," which was made by rolling a blob of molten glass in crushed glass (shot), then blowing into shape. Surface is very rough to touch. Shown is variant of Tree of Life.*

No. 180 – STEPPED HEXAGONS – Clear flint of the 50s shown in my Booklet 6. Evidently, one piece of a set. Covered sugar $80.00.

No. 10 – SANDWICH OVERSHOT – Overshot can always be told by the fact that is is so rough and sharp to the touch that it almost cuts one's fingers. Goblet $95.00. From the collection of Mrs. Kenneth Wakefield, on the Cape in Mass.

No. 184 – RAY – Clear flint. L. 14 and 163. Mrs. Lee stated it was made in Pittsburgh in the 50s and again in the late 60s. No goblet nor tumbler has been found so the pattern is not too much in demand. Tall celery $110.00; 6" plate, bowls, rectangular dish 5" x 7" $45.00; covered sugar $65.00; open sugar $35.00.

No. 93 – TINY LONG STAR – Heretofore unlisted. A lovely, clear flint of the 60s which I found up in Maine. I've never seen another piece although doubtless they existed. Celery $75.00.

The pieces found with gilt and twinning snakes are generally considered American, but they show many characteristics of English glass of the same era.

441
Knob Stem
Smocking

441
Smocking
Covered Sugar

440
Trimmed Smocking
Covered Sugar

442
Lined Smocking

447
Divided Diamonds

253
Dia. with Dia. Tipped Prisms

252
Lattice and Oval
Panels

252
Lattice and Oval
Panels

No. 441 – SMOCKING – L.V. 25-Mck., pl. 207 – Mil.-2 calls it PLAIN SMOCKING. Heavy flint of the 40s, fragments of which were found at the Sandwich factory site. The creamer is especially handsome with its applied handle and the top extending outward. Goblet, straight stem $70.00; knob stem $95.00; covered sugar or creamer $110.00; water pitcher $250.00; spill holder or spooner $50.00; egg cup $40.00; footed tumbler $40.00.

No. 441 – KNOB STEM SMOCKING – This is a very early form of smocking; goblet $90.00.

No. 440 – TRIMMED SMOCKING – This is probably another form of the same family, possibly put out by another factory at about the same time. Same values. On page 36 Book 1, Mrs. Kamm lists a creamer as English Pointed Thumbprint stating it was made there. I doubt it. One can't tell as much from the line drawings as from a photo, but I shouldn't be surprised if this were the creamer to our Smocking, shown here. This Smocking was listed for the first time in my Booklet 1.

No. 442 – LINED SMOCKING – Mil.-2. In this one, one can plainly see the horizontal lines crossing the sulci. Note the thick heavy stem. Clear flint of the 40s. Goblet $95.00.

No. 447 – DIVIDED DIAMONDS – Mil. Bk. 2-6. Almost another Smocking; the sulci are slightly more angular and are divided by vertical lines in this. Clear flint of the 50s. Goblet $85.00.

No. 253 – DIAMONDS AND DIAMOND-TIPPED PRISMS – Heretofore unlisted, save for my Booklet 6, clear and frosted flint of the early 60s. Most attractive. Goblet $125.00.

No. 252 – LATTICE AND OVAL PANELS – Mil. 81–L.V. calls it FLAT DIAMOND AND PANEL. Listed, but not pictured in my first book. The goblet is from the Dr. Bruce Swift collection. The pitcher from the Sandwich Museum. Goblet now $200.00; egg $65.00; wine $95.00; covered sugar $175.00; creamer $175.00; egg cup, covered $300.00; in color or opalescent $500.00 – 750.00. Such has been the story of the price of all good flint glass. *Boston & Sandwich Glass Co.*

HOW TO USE THIS BOOK

In the first place read, just because this book contains so many pictures don't think of it as a picture book, as the teens say, "Act you age," which in this case means be mature and read thoroughly and thoughtfully. It makes great difference whether glass is flint or lime glass and if flint I always state so, if not stated it is non-flint. How can one tell. Hold the object by the base and tap with a pencil, flint glass will ring, the more lead the more bell like the tone. This can help you date it, roughly. Lime glass was not invented until the 60s when the Civil War had caused a shortage of lead, so much being used as bullets.

At time a small variation in a pattern may change its value. This is due to a collector's reaction, for instance in one goblet you'll find a vast difference in price between the angular and the "u" shaped bowl, while there is no difference in value of goblet if it has round or angular base. How do you know? Read. Reread.

Champagne   Goblet
264
Early Double Vine

264
Early Double Vine

703
Clear Magnolia

796
Flower & Quill

706
Later Double Vine

291   292
Goblet   Champagne
Bellflower—Both Fine Rib
Base—plain—Base Rayed
Both Knob Stem

287
Bellflower with Loops

622
Daisy and Bluebell

54

No. 264 – EARLY DOUBLE VINE – Millard used this as a frontispiece to Book 2; Mrs. Lee–187 large plate below (706) as DOUBLE VINE, so I've added the word "EARLY" to name. I listed it in my first book and pictured it in my Booklet No. 6. I've warned against being a picture reader and skipping text. This goblet is a clear flint, probably of the 40s, rare and in great demand. Goblet $500.00; champagne $600.00; wine $450.00; tumbler $300.00; celery $400.00; decanter with original stopper $600.00. *Commonly known as Cut Bellflower, it was Fine Rib with cuttings. Boston & Sandwich Glass Co.*

No. 706 – LATER DOUBLE VINE PLATE – L.-187. Clear non-flint of the 70s. I've now seen this in the flat relish showing there was a setting. Flat relish $12.00; large plate $26.00.

No. 291 – BELLFLOWER-BARREL SHAPE-FINE RIB-PLAIN BASE – Clear, fine flint of the forties. Much more BELLFLOWER listed in my first book. This type goblet $65.00.

No. 292 – BELLFLOWER-FINE RIB-KNOB STEM-RAYED BASE – Another fine type of the early Bellflower. Champagne shown for comparison in size. Champagne $175.00; goblet $75.00. All fine rib Bellflower is much more desirable than the coarse rib.

No. 287 – BELLFLOWER WITH LOOPS – Mil. Bk. 2-87. A very fine very scarce and sought after goblet in fine ribs of course. Goblet $350.00.

No. 703 – CLEAR MAGNOLIA – This has been listed by Millard, Kamm and in my first book in Frosted, but my Booklet 1 was the first listing in clear; and this is one of the extremely few patterns which are more valuable in clear than in frosted form. Goblet, clear $60.00; clear cakestand $90.00. This is a non-flint pattern of the 70s or early 80s.

No. 796 – FLOWER AND QUILL – (PRETTY BAND) – When I first found this I thought it to be unlisted and called it the second name, but later I found it in K. Bk. 3-52 called by first name, and there is no reason to change that pretty title, so I used it in Booklet 4, where I show the insert to the pickle castor, a square piece, as all of the upright pieces were. Clear non-flint of mid 80s. Value of pickle castor depends largely on condition of plated container, from $60.00; open pickle, no silver container $10.00; creamer $25.00.

No. 622 – DAISY AND BLUEBELL – K. Bk. 1-9. Clear, non-flint of the 80s. Attractive floral probably made in setting. Creamer $25.00.

385
Panelled Fern

871
Oval Panelled
Frosted Grape

1003
Flower Medallion

1687
Dodo

87
Elm Leaf

1697
Hawaiian Pineapple

1178
Arched Leaf Plate

267
Sawtooth Circle Salt

No. 385 – PANELLED FERN – I believe the goblet listed by Millard – Bk. 2-39 and which he calls HAMMOND is this one, but the picture is so indistinct that it is impossible to tell. I'm giving it the name by which it is known in the neighborhood of Sandwich where it is well known. It is no relation to the late non-flint that Mrs. Kamm – (Bk. 5-43) mentions. It is clear flint of the 50s found in several pieces in that locale, some of which are shown in the Sandwich Museum. Goblet $50.00; wine $35.00; open sugar $25.00; covered sugar $65.00; creamer $55.00.

No. 871 – OVAL PANELLED FROSTED GRAPE – Previously unlisted, clear and frosted flint glass of the 50s. This exceptionally fine giblet is in the Sandwich Museum. It seems to be a relative of the lovely Magnet and Grape with Frosted Leaf, but this one is much scarcer. Goblet $260.00.

No. 1003 – FLOWER MEDALLION – When I first reported this in my Booklet 5, I had seen only the non-flint version. Now I've seen it in flint same as shown and also with small added etched geometric band about one-half inch from the top. Flint goblet $75.00; non-flint one $45.00. The flint was probably made in the late 60s and the non-flint on into the 70s. Etchings does not change the value.

No. 1687 – DODO – M.-40 – K. Bk. 8-70 calls it TRIANGULAR MEDALLION. I prefer the latter more descriptive name. It was first known by the senseless listing, however. Clear flint of mid 60s; goblet $45.00.

No. 1697 – HAWAIIAN PINEAPPLE – Mil. – 12. Clear flint of the late 60s or early 70s. Goblet $195.00; tumbler $150.00.

No. 1178 – ARCHED LEAF – 11" plate shown; listed but not pictured in my first book. This plate in flint $35.00; colors, rare $60.00. *Generally found in non-flint. Plate sits on little knobs.*

No. 87 – ELM LEAF – Heretofore unlisted. Shallow, clear, rather heavy flint bowl, early characteristic, probably the 50s, which I found in the Nickerson collection on the Cape. Bowl shown $40.00.

No. 267 – SAWTOOTH CIRCLE SALT – Shown in my Booklet 4. I'm frequently shown this salt in the mid-west with the query, "Is this Sandwich?" I doubt it as I don't find it there as we do in the mid-west; possibly midwestern. Clear flint salt of the late 60s $30.00.

55
Loop and Ovals

305
Plain Tulip

306
Double Petal Tulip

300
Small Flowered Tulip

38
Climbing Ivy Spill

37
Armorial Spill

40
Arch Band Spill

41
Two Way Heart Spill

No.55 – LOOP AND OVALS – Mil. Bk. 2-26. Clear flint of the 60s. Goblet $60.00.

NO. 305 – PLAIN TULIP – Wine shown in my first book, shown here for comparison with No. 306 below. Clear flint of the 60s; wine, now $45.00; goblet $75.00.

No. 306 – DOUBLE PETAL TULIP – Listed, but not pictured, in my first book. Very like its contemporary, No. 305 above, only this has another row of petals extending up about one-third of the way of the bowl and of the goblet and seemingly over the first row. Some values as above.

No. 300 – SMALL FLOWERED TULIP WITH RIBS – Heretofore unlisted, clear flint of the 60s. Very like Small Flowered Tulip, 299, shown in my first book, only that has sawteeth while one listed here has ribs. I suspect it was made in sets as Tulip and Sawtooth were but the goblet is all that has been found so far. Flint goblet $75.00. Other pieces would have the same value as that of the Tulip and Sawtooth. *Mug $45.00, 200% more for cobalt.*

No. 38 – CLIMBING IVY SPILL – This flint spill of the 50s, one of four shown here is part of collection of Mrs. Kenneth Wakefield of Mass. Heretofore unlisted. Spill $100.00. *Sandwich.*

No. 37 – ARMORIAL SPILL – Another spill from Mrs. Wakefield's collection. Clear flint, $100.00. Heretofore unlisted. These spills may date even prior to 50s we know not. We're only certain they are very early.

No. 40 – ARCH BAND SPILL – This one is shown, but not named in L.V.-78. I've given them names to help in identification. Same age and values as others.

No. 41 – TWO WAY HEART SPILL – Also shown in L.V.-78. Same age and values as others.

TWO TRUTHS CULLED FROM THE PRESS

The Superintendent of Schools of New York City, "Every citizen of this country, whether he pounds nails, raises corn, designs rockets or writes poetry should be taught to know and to love the American heritage. The dollars he earns, in the absence of an enlightenment like this, will be earned in drudgery and spent in ignorance."

And at last I found this definition, "Art is the human making of things, skillfully."

Notes: Spills are often found in the same patterns as early lamps. They were used to hold slivers of wood or rolled paper to transfer a flame for lighting lamps before safety matches were common. Later spills were reused as spooners and will be found with small chips inside from the metal spoons. Spills will have the same shape as those shown and be flint.

678
Clover and Daisy

678
Clover & Daisy
Other Side

681
Cranesbill

9
Sandwich Vine

774
Panelled Wild Daisy

777
Fern Sprig

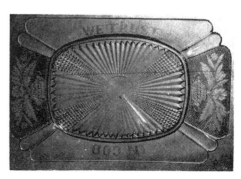

642
Flower Pot Bread Tray

No. 678 – CLOVER AND DAISY – Mil.-116. Clear, non-flint of the 80s. Two views of the goblet shown. The only specimen which I've seen is a poor quality glass, greyed one with the unfinished tell-tale line of the goblet used to sell jelly in. The design is attractive, and if the quality of the glass were better the goblet would be in demand. A book to be of use to the novice collector should warn him of these facts; frequently they do not show in either photo or line drawing. Poor quality glass goblet $25.00; if glass were clear, the goblet would be worth $35.00. I show this one in my Booklet No. 4.

No. 681 – CRANESBILL – K. Bk. 1-62 – Mrs. Kamm tells us that the cranesbill is another name for the wild geranium which this pattern depicts. It seems each author has his contribution to make to help our glass knowledge. In Mrs. Kamm's case, it is the terminology in these naturalistic patterns as she had her doctorate in biology and was accurate in naming our flora and fauna. The sugar of this seems to be rather carelessly and strangely made, the design in the top and in the base run in differing directions and vary slightly in detail; another difference, not too unusual, is that on the base design is on the outside, on the cover, on the inside of the dish. A clear, non-flint of the 80s, probably the work of one of the smaller factories. Covered sugar $35.00; creamer $25.00; there must be more.

No. 9 – SANDWICH VINE – Here is the goblet used as a frontispiece in my first book, only here it has a gilt top. The dealer from whom I got my first goblet in these, told a story, which I'm sure she believed that they were part of the glass of the Deming Jarves family, made for them and never sold beyond the family. She offered to give me written proof. The goblet was lovely and early, and I care not for stories.

Needless to say the dear lady has passed on. The story's proof never came and I've found more on the cape, near Sandwich. I believe they were made there but this family story is entirely fictional, I'm convinced, and adds nothing to quality of the goblet. Goblet now $1,500.00+. *One sold at auction in 1998 for $10,000.00.*

No. 774 – PANELLED WILD DAISY – K. Bk. 3-66 calls it PANELLED SUNFLOWER but as we have another goblet by that name, I prefer to use the foregoing name of Mil.-106. Clear and stippled, non-flint of the 70s, shown in my Booklet No. 4. A very pleasing effect is obtained by the stippling of alternate leaves and petals. Covered butter $25.00; covered sugar $25.00; goblet $15.00; covered compote $30.00.

No. 777 – FERN SPRIG – Listed but not pictured in my first book, shown in my Booklet No. 3. Goblet $20.00; covered butter $25.00; covered sugar $25.00. Mil. Bk. 2-163.

No. 642 – FLOWER POT – Listed but not pictured in my first book. This bread tray now $45.00; sauce $8.00; creamer $25.00; covered sugar $40.00.

Note: Goblets such as #678 with a straight rim and made of inferior glass were probably sold for use as jelly glasses, as seen in some catalogs of the time. They would have had a slip-on metal lid.

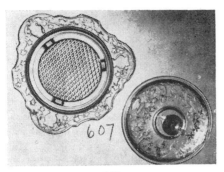

607
Twinkle Phlox

578
Rose Sprig Sleigh Salt

1224
Hundred Leaved Ivy

582
Rose Branches

739
Daisy Drape

669
Stippled Woodflower

9" Kitten Plate

7" Baby Plate

596
Stippled Forget-me-not

No. 607 – TWINKLE PHLOX – Previously unlisted; blue non-flint covered butter dish in charming floral design. I've seen another in clear; this one is from the collection of the Melvilles of Colgate, Wisconsin, whose collection is well worth seeing. Butter dish in clear $45.00; in blue, shown $65.00.

No. 1224 – HUNDRED LEAVED IVY – Listed in my first book. Lee 115 listed flat sauce in this as CAPE COD, and I know this was an error for I had seen the large plate and it was not the Cape Cod plate. This butter dish is in the Sandwich Museum. Butter dish $55.00. *Aka Panelled Ivy.*

No. 578 – ROSE SPRIG – Listed in my first book, but this is the tiny sleigh salt in yellow from the Sandwich Museum. It is now rare; yellow sleigh salt $75.00; *also blue, amber, clear 40% less. Some marked "1888" although patented 1886 for Campbell, Jones of Pittsburgh, PA. Reproduced.*

No. 582 – ROSE BRANCHES – Previously unlisted, clear, non-flint of the 70s. I've had sketches of creamer sent to me for identification purposes but have heard of nothing save the covered sugar $45.00; creamer $25.00. There must be more.

No. 739 – DAISY DRAPE – Another heretofore unlisted attractive conventionalized floral and the interesting thing is that the finial on this butter is exactly the same as the unusual handle urn type on 607 above. The picture is somewhat misleading. The base of butter is square due to fans on flange of each corner. Clear, non-flint of the 70s; covered butter $50.00.

No. 669 – STIPPLED WOODFLOWER – Clear, stippled, non-flint of the 70s. Covered sugar has most interesting, single upright leaf finial. Seldom seen. Creamer from Sandwich Museum. Covered sugar $50.00; creamer $30.00.

No. 596 – STIPPLED FORGET-ME-NOT 7" BABY CENTER PLATE – Pattern shown in my first book, but this scarce plate frequently is not recognized. Plate now $80.00. *Can be found in amber, blue, opal (milk) 80% more. Findlay Glass Co. 1890.*

No. 596 – STIPPLED FORGET-ME-NOT 9" KITTEN CENTER PLATE – Another rare plate of this family. Plate $80.00. Above two plates are from Sandwich Museum. *Findlay Glass Co., 1889. Similar plates with star center 25% less, also in colors, 50% more.*

2607
Horsemint

850
Phytolacca

822
Pampas Flower

1709
Near **Garland**

775
Girl with Flower

966
Inverted Strawberry

747
Late Thistle

674
Lacy Daisy

No. 2607 – HORSEMINT – Mil. Bk. 2-22. Clear, non-flint of the 90s, reflecting the image of the imitation cut glass coming out and so popular in cheaper stores at this time. Goblet $20.00; wine $20.00.

No. 850 – PHYTOLACCA – M. Bk. 2-105. Clear, non-flint of the late 80s or early 90s. Note very fancy stem and design of both geometric and floral units. Goblet $25.00.

No. 822 – PAMPAS FLOWER – K. Bk. 4-12. Clear, non-flint of the 80s, trimmed with band of stippling outlined with tiny dots. Open sugar shown $12.00; footed sauce $10.00; creamer $30.00; should be a setting; *covered sugar $45.00.*

No. 674 – LACY DAISY – K. Bk. 2-73 – 1 L.-44 calls it simply DAISY. Listed in my book, but this is a scarce piece in the pattern not often seen; mustard, shown $60.00; tall open jelly compote $60.00. *J.B. Higbee, 1908; New Martinsville, 1916. Reproduced by Westmoreland 1940s.*

No. 966 – INVERTED STRAWBERRY – Listed but not pictured in my first book. Goblet $125.00; plate not $50.00; reproduced in clear and color. *Occasionally found ruby stained and emerald green, 100% more. Cambridge Glass #2870, 1915.*

No. 747 – *INVERTED THISTLE* – L. 187 – K. Bk. 1-3. Listed but not pictured in my first book; attractive and in demand, marked "near-cut" plate shown $50.00; tumbler $45.00; covered sugar $45.00; water or milk pitcher $75.00. *Occasionally found in emerald green and carnival. Cambridge, 1906. Imperial Glass Co. reproduced in 1960s in clear and colors.*

No. 1709 – NEAR GARLAND – I believe this pattern was the one from which the designer obtained his motif for GARLAND, Mil. Bk. 2-131. This is earlier, in Garland the design is simpler of course; most pieces carry only the border motif. Frequently platters and cheese dishes carried other scenes. The center of the tray, a clear, non-flint of the 70s is about 1" deep and is probably one of the ice cream trays so popular at that time. Tray shown $60.00. *Central Glass #585, covered sugar (dog finial) $95.00. Aka LEAFLETS.*

No. 775 – GIRL WITH FLOWERS – Heretofore unlisted, clear, non-flint of the mid 70s with design put on in the same way as on the Cupid and Psyche pattern. This 4½" footed sauce is the only piece I've ever seen, but there must be more. Sauce $15.00; *jelly $45.00; low footed bowl $45.00.*

591
Panelled
Wee Blossoms

911
Small Wild Grape

588
Campanula

724
Panelled Dogwood

707
Frosted Flower Band

715
Round Marsh
Pink

589
Columbine

819
Chrysanthemum
Leaf

No. 591 – PANELLED WEE BLOSSOMS – Amber, non-flint goblet of the 80s from the collection of the Willard Melvilles of Colgate, Wisconsin. Undoubtedly this would also be found in clear $30.00; amber $40.00. Not previously listed.

No. 911 – SMALL WILD GRAPE – Heretofore unlisted. Lovely blue grape form, probably of the late 60s, also from the splendid Melville collection. The endless way in which the grape motif was treated in old glass is a never ending source of pleasure. Blue goblet $150.00; clear would be $95.00.

No. 588 – CAMPANULA – Clear and stippled, non-flint of the 70s. While goblet takes a pretty picture, the goblet in real life, is rather ordinary, of mediocre quality $35.00; *butter $45.00; covered sugar $40.00; creamer $35.00; spooner $30.00; goblet $35.00.*

No. 724 – PANELLED DOGWOOD – Mil. Bk. 2-114 and on plate 36 he shows it with flowers and leaves painted; K-Bk.-1-69 shows the painted variety calling it simply DOG-WOOD. The color adds nothing to it. *Good color is presently very desirable, making item 50% more valuable.* Non-flint of the late 80s, probably made in sets; goblet $25.00; creamer $30.00. *Cooperative Flint, 1903; U.S. Glass, 1919. Aka ART NOVO.*

No. 707 – FROSTED FLOWER BAND – Listed and goblet pictured in my first book. The picture of the sugar is shown here because it is such an important piece with its love birds finial and is so seldom seen. This one is from the Sandwich Museum. Greatly in demand and prices have skyrocketed; covered sugar $110.00; creamer $85.00; goblet $95.00. *Reproduced in clear and colors not original. Aka Flower Band.*

No. 708 – FROSTED OAK BAND – (not pictured, listed in my book) I stated it was made only in goblet. Since then I've seen other pieces showing that it too, was made in sets. *10% more than Flower Band.*

No. 715 – ROUND MARSH PINK – Heretofore unlisted, scarce member of the Marsh Pink family. I show the Square in my first book. Differs not only in shape but in the stippled band around the top. Clear, non-flint of the 80s. Goblet $125.00; *plate $20.00; sauce $12.00. Aka Bay St. Louis.*

No. 589 – COLUMBINE – Clear, non-flint of the 80s. Goblet from the Swift collection in the Allen Museum. Goblet $90.00. A set of these flower goblets would be charming.

No. 819 – CHRYSANTHEMUM LEAF – L.V. 19. Clear, non-flint of the late 80s. Seldom seen. Vase shown, from Sandwich Museum. Flat sauce $15.00; bowl, spooner, sherbet cup $35.00; vase $45.00; tumbler $45.00; butter $65.00; creamer $50.00. *Made by Boston Sandwich Glass in 1880s; chocolate 350% more; ruby stained 200% more. Chocolate made after 1901 by National Glass or McKee.*

1401
Rosette & Palms

1435
Panelled Palm

1778
Gypsy

1688
Tiawanna

1434
Palm & Scroll

1001
Wreath and Bar

718
Circled Scroll

No. 1401 – ROSETTE AND PALMS – Listed in my first book and pictured in Booklet No. 5. Clear, non-flint, prices of which have advanced rather sharply. Now, open sugar $20.00; spooner $25.00; flat sauce dish $18.00; relish dish $20.00; 8" plate $20.00; goblet $35.00; wine $25.00; open compote $30.00; 10" plate $25.00; celery $30.00; butter $50.00; cakestand $40.00; covered compote $45.00; covered sugar $40.00; creamer $35.00; water pitcher $50.00. *Bryce Higbee, 1905. J.B. Higbee, 1907.*

No. 1434 – PALM AND SCROLL – Mil. Bk. 2-51-K. Bk. 2-113, listed and pictured in by Booklet No. 1. Kamm calls it PALM LEAF AND SCROLL. Clear and a few pieces in dark green, *blue*, canary and amethyst made by one of the U.S. Glass Co.'s factories, probably in the *late* 90s after the merger. Most pieces in clear are not in too great demand with the exception of the goblet which is extremely difficult to find. The design is as pleasing as many of the earlier non-flints. Covered sugar $55.00; covered butter $65.00; creamer $35.00; goblet $75.00. This is due to the fact that the many goblet hunters are after it for their collections. *Missouri preferred name. Emerald green 50% more; other colors 300% more. Cakestand $65.00; open compote $40.00; covered compote $70.00; pitcher $75.00; syrup $95.00; wine $55.00.*

No. 1435 – PANELLED PALM – M. Bk. 2-37 – Clear and clear with colored panels, non-flint of the early 90s. It is the background of the panels which are at times found in yellow, red or amethyst. Clear goblet $20.00; any color $30.00; all non-flint. *Aka Brilliant, U.S. Glass #15095, 1906.*

No. 1778 – GYPSY – Mil. 140. Clear, non-flint of the 80s. Only goblet found so far, value $20.00.

No. 1688 – TIAWANNA – Mil.-27. Clear, non-flint of the 80s. To date, only goblet, $20.00.

No. 718 – CIRCLED SCROLL – K. Bk. 4-70. Clear, canary, blue, green with opalescent edge and trim, attractive and simple in design and opalescence is handled well. Clear sauce $40.00; open sugar $60.00; creamer $90.00; berry bowl $120.00; covered sugar $135.00; tumbler $55.00. *Canary 100% more, blue 60% more, green 50% more. Northwood, 1903. No goblet.*

No. 717 – LEAFY SCROLL – (Not pictured). Another member of the Circled Scroll family above, very much like it only in this the creamer for instance, is all upright pieces, becomes smaller toward the top and is joined to a plain band, encircling the top. There is also a continuing line from one scroll to another. Has some of the merit of earlier ware and its small size adapts it to small homes of today. Tankard type water pitcher $45.00; cakestand $50.00; cracker jar $60.00; *goblet $35.00*. Other pieces same value as Circled Scroll. *U.S. Glass #15034, 1896.*

No. 1001 – WREATH AND BARS – Mil. Bk. 2-6. Clear non-flint of the late 70s or early 80s. Looped garlands of leaves ending in tiny flowers are separated into three groups by triple vertical lines. Goblet in demand by goblet collectors $30.00. Must be other pieces.

1389
Corner Medallion

1389
Corner Medallion

1386
Aida

1390
Leaf Medallion

1387
Bamboo Edge—Side

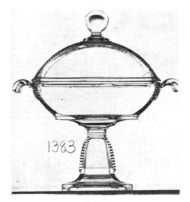

1383
Center Medallion Side

1383
End
Center Medallion

1387
Ends

70

No. 1389 – CORNER MEDALLION – Unlisted until noted in my Booklet No. 2. Clear, non-flint of the 80s; made in four piece set and probably compotes and other pieces. Second picture shows the decor on ends of pieces. Spooner $20.00; creamer $30.00; open compote $25.00; sugar $35.00; footed sauce $80.00; covered compote $60.00. Front view and side view of creamer shown. *Central Glass #720, 1880.*

No. 1386 – AIDA – K. Bk. 5-20 suggests this was the original name of this pattern. Open sugar shown. These fancy names belong to an era of our country when, in some section, "get culture quick," seemed to be the watchword so even glass had to be named for an opera. Clear non-flint, contemporary of Corner Medallion and values are the same. Etched or not does not change price. *Belmont Glass, c 1883.*

No. 1390 – LEAF MEDALLION – First listed in my Booklet No. 2. Clear, non-flint of the 80s and another relative, a cousin, probably, of the above family. The medallion is somewhat like the one on the base of Bamboo Edge, but it differs in outline. Creamer is smaller than the others though larger than individual size. Creamer $20.00. *Not to be confused with Northwood's Regent which is sometimes called Leaf Medallion also.*

No. 1387 – BAMBOO EDGE – K. Bk. 5-21 calls this BAMBOO, but as there is an entirely different pattern with that name I'm adding the descriptive word. One form of etching, a wheat sheaf, is really pleasing but the pattern is too busy to have anything added to it. Comes in many pieces; spooner $30.00; rectangular relishes, three sizes $12.00 – 20.00; open sugar $20.00; pair of salt shakers $60.00; covered butter $50.00; covered sugar $45.00; footed sauce dish $10.00; open compotes $20.00; covered compotes three sizes $45.00 – 75.00. Etching does not change value. *Variation on the Grace or Japanese pattern. LaBelle Glass Co., c 1883.*

No. 1383 – CENTER MEDALLION – First listed in my Booklet No. 2. Clear, non-flint of the early 80s and another of the family of Corner Medallion and Bamboo Edge. End and side view of tall covered compote shown. I suppose the same pieces were made in this as were made in the other members of the family but this is all I've seen in this up to now. Values would be the same as for Bamboo Edge. It has been called Shawl but I can't see a shawl standing erect and stiff as this design does. *U.S. Glass, 1905.*

792
Oak Leaf Band

784
Oak Wreath

795
Beaded Acorn
with Leaf Band

798
Pressed Leaf with Chain

799
Crossed Pressed Leaf

793
Oak Leak Band with Loops

283
Curved Stem Acorn

800
Birch Leaf

72

No. 792 – OAK LEAF BAND – Mil. Bk. 2-13, shown in my Booklet No. 1, clear, non-flint of the 70s. Goblet $50.00; wine $35.00; creamer $35.00; covered sugar $45.00; celery $40.00; footed master salt $15.00. Goblet now reproduced. *Central Glass #99 c 1880; U.S. Glass, 1891.*

No. 784 – OAK WREATH – K. Bk. 6-5. At first glance this appears to be another factory's interpretation of 792 above, but other pieces in the set vary so much that it is definitely another pattern. The master salt is flat and oval; the goblet is much smaller and is not as husky looking. It is same age and same value as Oak Leaf Band. *Central Glass, 1880s; U.S. Glass, 1890s.*

No. 795 – BEADED ACORN WITH LEAF BAND – Mil. Bk. 2-10. Listed in my first book and pictured in my Booklet No. 6. I've now seen a flint goblet in this. Goblet, non-flint $35.00; flint $50.00. *Aka Oak Leaf Band with Medallion; reported to be Portland Glass Co.*

No. 810 – ACORN IN WREATH – Previously unlisted (Not pictured). The only place I've ever seen this goblet is in the goblet collection in the Bennington Museum. It has the band of leaves above, and the lower part of the goblet bowl is separated by acanthus like leaves into panels. In each of these three panels are wreaths, in which there are acorns. Needless to say, it is scarce. Goblet $125.00.

No. 798 – PRESSED LEAF WITH CHAIN – Mil. Bk. 2-10. Clear, non-flint of the 70s shown in my Booklet No. 6; values same as Oak Leaf Band.

No. 799 – CROSSED PRESSED LEAF – Mil.-164. Clear, non-flint of the late 60s, early 70s. Millard lists this as of the 80s, but I think the pitcher proves it earlier than that. Shown in my Booklet No. 6. Values same as Oak Leaf Band. *Goblet $35.00; Aka Crossed Leaf.*

No. 793 – OAK LEAF BAND WITH LOOPS – Mil. Bk. 2-43. Clear non-flint of the early 70s; listed under Oak Leaf Band with Prisms instead of this correct title in my Booklet No. 6. Values same as Oak Leaf Band.

No. 283 – CURVED STEM ACORN – Heretofore unlisted, rare, clear flint of the 50s found, so far, only in wine shown. Heavy, early glass and rare; wine $50.00. I'd like to hear of more of it.

No. 800 – BIRCH LEAF – Clear non-flint and flint, also found in milk white. Wine $30.00; goblet $40.00; egg cup $20.00; spooner $20.00; in flint or milk glass an additional 100%.

279
Ribbed Acorn

742
Southern Ivy

738
Stippled Ivy

741
Spiralled Ivy

629
Bleeding Heart

1643

1643

Quatrefoil **Covered** Sugar and Creamer

No. 279 – RIBBED ACORN – L. 39. Clear flint of the 30s or 40s, extremely scarce. Covered butter shown is from the Nickerson collection. A cousin and contemporary of the Bellflower pattern, but probably made over a much shorter period of years because so little of it has come to light. Covered butter $85.00; low 6" covered compote $80.00; sweetmeat dish (6" tall covered compote) $90.00; honey or sauce dish $20.00; open compote $50.00; with scalloped edge $65.00. *Attributed to Boston & Sandwich, 1850.*

No. 742 – SOUTHERN IVY – L. 166 – While this is a ribbed pattern it is a later, non-flint and does not belong to the same family as the early flint ribbed patterns do. Egg cup $15.00; berry bowl $20.00; sauce dish $5.00; covered sugar $30.00; tumbler $25.00; water pitcher $45.00. It is most important that collectors distinguish between the flint and non-flint; a reader sent me a sketch of the water pitcher in this, thinking she had a prize, she must have been disappointed when I told her the cold truth. *Mug $20.00.*

No. 738 – STIPPLED IVY – Listed but not pictured in my first book, but pictured in Booklet No. 4. Clear, non-flint of the 70s, very like Budded Ivy with the exception that the latter has the added buds. Pitchers have applied handles and the finials are most interesting upright leaves of ivy. Flat sauce or honey dish $6.00; footed master salt $20.00; egg cup $15.00; spooner $20.00; open sugar $20.00; covered butter $35.00; open compote $25.00; creamer, covered sugar $30.00; goblet $30.00; wine $25.00; tall covered compote $50.00.

No. 741 – SPIRALLED IVY – L. 147. Listed, but not pictured in my first book, shown in Booklet No. 4. A relative to Southern Ivy of which it is a contemporary and likewise never popular, possibly because there was no goblet. The tumbler has advanced in price as have all tumblers due to their present popularity for serving "Old Fashions," etc. Tumblers, now $30.00; *creamer $25.00.*

No. 629 – BLEEDING HEART – Aka Floral. L. 128 shows this creamer with later type handle and later, not bulbous form. Evidently it was made over a long period of years; we find different qualities in the goblets and there are most certainly different qualities in the creamers. It was probably made from the late 60s even as late and the 80s. Creamer of this quality $95.00; fine clear knob stem goblet now $55.00. *King Glass Co. #85 c 1875. Specialty Glass made poor quality goblets and mugs. One type of goblet was a jelly container. It has an indistinct impression and glass quality is poorer. Aka Floral.*

No. 1643 – QUATREFOIL – Listed in my first book and as a result these pictures were sent to me from Ohio. No goblet nor tumbler has yet been found which limits use of set for table service, however the individual pieces have enough charm to use as single decorative units. Covered butter $45.00; creamer $30.00; covered sugar $35.00; covered compote $40.00; open compotes $20.00.

928
Beaded Grape

916
Medallion

913
Grape Bunch

917
Grape Toothpick

1152
Frosted Artichoke

914
Grape with
Scroll Medallion

1008
Frosted Fruits

931
Pear

857
Pea Pods

No. 928 – BEADED GRAPE – This is listed on page 83 in my first book; the index was incorrect. MARKET FLOODED WITH REPRODUCTIONS. When Mrs. Lee was writing her *Fakes and Reproductions* some years ago, she and I looked all over for months, then she borrowed one from a collection. One shown is from Swift collection in Allen Museum in Oberlin, Ohio. Pattern reproduced in all pieces, in both clear and green. *Aka California. Goblet $45.00; butter $40.00.*

No. 916 – BEADED GRAPE MEDALLION – Also listed, but not pictured on page 83 in my first book. Goblet $40.00.

No. 913 – GRAPE BUNCH – Previously unlisted, non-flint egg from the Sandwich Museum. Value $12.00. It resembles the new Leaf egg cup which I show in the "NO, NO'S" in my first book. On careful inspection one sees more careful modelling here and, of course, this has the added bunch of grapes. There probably was a setting of Grape Bunch. *Probably Greentown about 1900. Originally a container.*

No. 917 – GRAPE TOOTHPICK – 2¼" tall, clear, unlisted non-flint of the 70s; one of the earlier novelties. Toothpick $25.00.

No. 1152 – FROSTED ARTICHOKE – Listed but not pictured in my first book. Finger bowl and matching plate $45.00 set. Remember, goblet is reproduction — **not** made originally. Fostoria Glass Co., #205 c 1891.

No. 914 – GRAPE WITH SCROLL MEDALLION – K. Bk. 2-56. Interesting non-flint of the early 70s; clear only. Covered sugar, grape bunch finial $30.00; creamer $25.00; covered butter $45.00; spooner $25.00; open sugar shown $15.00; water pitcher $45.00.

No. 1008 – FROSTED FRUITS – Pictured in my first book, but bowl pictured did not lend itself to satisfactory picture. Many not recognizing pattern have sent me rubbings of "this beautiful pitcher." It is just that, water pitcher $90.00 in clear and frosted.

No. 931 – PEAR – L.V.-72. Listed in my first book and shown in my Booklet No. 1. Mil. -59, calls it BARTLETT PEAR. I can't see why one would want to collect the oft reproduced Baltimore Pear when there is this better, slightly older one. Finials of covered pieces are acorns. Flat sauce $6.00; open sugar $15.00; spooner $25.00; goblet $40.00; covered sugar $45.00; creamer $30.00. *George Duncan & Sons, c 1885.*

No. 857 – PEA PODS – Previously unlisted, clear, non-flint pattern of the 70s and a most interesting pattern, of fine design. Milk pitcher shown $45.00.

961
Dunlop Strawberry

962
Falmouth Strawberry

979
Blackberry Band

1151
Melon

1143
Pineapple

910
Bradford
Grape

916
Beaded Grape Medallion

No. 961 – DUNLOP STRAWBERRY – Mil. 60. Clear, non-flint of the 70s. Goblet $35.00; shown in my Booklet No. 6.

No. 962 – FALMOUTH STRAWBERRY – Mil. Bk. 2-39. Later than Dunlop above as shown by additional fussiness of design, of late 80s or early 90s; goblet $45.00.

No. 963 – GANDY STRAWBERRY – Mil. 60 (not pictured). Larger than Dunlop but otherwise quite similar except for narrow banding about 1" from top of goblet. Clear, non-flint of the 70s; goblet $30.00.

No. 979 – BLACKBERRY BAND – Mil. 62. Clear, non-flint of the 70s. Not to be confused with Grape Band which has the tendrils; this has none. Open sugar, often called "buttermilk" shown $25.00; covered sugar $45.00; creamer $35.00. There certainly are other pieces in the pattern. *OMN: DEWBERRY VINE, Belmont Glass c 1870s, patented April 12, 1870.*

No. 1151 – MELON – L. 181 shows this piece which is really the covered sugar. Non-flint of the late 70s or early 80s, which comes in clear, canary, amber, blue, and blue and white milk glass. Very interesting, all pieces in melon shapes; the larger melons are the compotes. Covered sugar $65.00; creamer (no cover) $45.00; larger melons $85.00 – 100.00; in milk glass or any color an added 30% – 50%. *Apparently, many strange colors were made originally. No evidence of reproductions. Made by Atterbury and patented 4/23/78, some pieces dated. Mug $60.00.*

No. 1143 – PINEAPPLE – L.V. 38. When I saw this pattern for the first time and showed it in my first book I was not impressed by it; it was mediocre in quality of glass and in modelling of the pineapple. Since then I've seen it in a beautiful, clear fine glass with perfectly formed pineapples protruding from the various dishes, and it is truly outstanding and rare. Prices for this quality are covered butter $55.00; covered sugar $60.00; creamer $40.00; tumbler $30.00; cakestand $75.00. It has been listed in milk white which would be worth an additional 30% if the modelling were fine. *Spooner $30.00.*

No. 910 – BRADFORD GRAPE – K. Bk. 5-25. L.V. 22 calls it BRADFORD BLACKBERRY but stem is woody and it has tendrils which seem to put it in the grape family. Shown in Booklet 1. Clear flint of early 60s. Wine $60.00; champagne $90.00; goblet $225.00; creamer $125.00; covered sugar $125.00. *Boston and Sandwich, c 1860.*

No. 916 – BEADED GRAPE MEDALLION – Base of bowl shown here. Pattern listed in my first book and goblet shown on previous page, but here is one of the few pattern dishes carrying its patent mark in the base, "Mould pat. May 11, 1869." A fine piece to have in any collection. This oval bowl originally had a cover $105.00; base $35.00. *Boston and Silver Glass Co. 1870, possibly the Boston and Sandwich Glass Co. after 1871 (Boston Silver closed in 1871).*

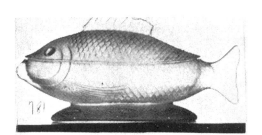

781
Fish Dish

778
Cow Covered Dish

1145
Butterfly Handles

779
Duck Geometric Base

1054
Pheasant Covered Dish

780
Duck Naturalistic Base

1109
Lone Elk

856
Deer and Oak Tree

No. 781– FISH COVERED DISH – There are several of these fish covered dishes, each varying slightly from the other. All are clear, non-flints of the 70s and are of the same value $125.00. *Central Glass #747.*

No. 779 – DUCK DISH WITH GEOMETRIC BASE – L.V.-114 classifies this one as rare. Value $110.00.

No. 780 – DUCK WITH NATURALISTIC BASE – L.V.-113. Contemporary, the 70s of duck above, both non-flint of the 70s, both about 7" long, only we meet this one a little more frequently. Value $90.00. These two handsome fellows plus the fine fish above swim across the shelf dividing my hopelessly long kitchen windows, and furnish me joy as they recall our bass fishing days with our boys, on the lake in Minnesota. *Central Glass #727.*

No. 778 – COW BUTTER DISH – Clear, non-flint of the 70s, about 6" long; value $140.00.

No. 1054 – PHEASANT COVERED BOWL – L. 99. Clear, non-flint, oval bowl with beautiful large pheasant on the cover. The modelling of the bird is unusually skillful as is true of many of these animal dishes of the 70s. From the Sandwich Museum. Value $220.00. *Central Glass #758. Reproduced by Imperial Glass,* c 1960s.

No. 1109 – LONE ELK – Clear and frosted, non-flint of the 70s which I found up in Maine. I've never seen nor heard of anything save this open sugar, value $45.00; if covered $95.00.

No. 1145 – BUTTERFLY HANDLES – L.V. calls it simply BUTTERFLY but as there is another pattern by that name I had to add to it. Listed but not pictured in my first book. All clear or clear with frosted handles (butterflies) and band; non-flint of the 80s. Prices now: oval pickle, handled, covered mustard $25.00; pair salt shakers $55.00; open sugar $20.00; spooner $30.00; covered butter $45.00; creamer $30.00; celery (pictured) $45.00; covered sugar $40.00.

No. 865 – BRINGING HOME THE COWS – Value $450.00 – 600.00. Not necessary to describe name does that. K. Bk. 4-125. *Dalzell, Gilmore, Leighton.*

No. 866 – GIRL WITH BICYCLE – Value $450.00 – 600.00. Bk. 5-126. *Aka Bicycle Girl. Dalzell, Gilmore, Leighton.*

No. 868 – DOG HUNTING – Value $300.00 – 400.00. K. Bk. 4-125.

No. 851 – THE FOX AND THE CROW – Value $300.00 – 400.00. K. Bk. 4-124. *Dalzell, Gilmore, Leighton.*

No. 1099 – DEER ALERT – Value $300.00 – 400.00. K. Bk. 4-124.

No. 856 – DEER AND OAK TREE – Same as above only in this, the oak tree covers most of the pitcher and the deer stands directly beneath the center of it. Value $300.00 – 400.00. K. Bk. 3-122. *Dalzell, Gilmore, Leighton.*

Note:

Indiana Tumbler and Goblet, Greentown, IN, did the following pitchers only:

	Clear	Chocolate
Racing Deer & Doe	$250.00	$650.00
Heron	250.00	800.00
Squirrel (Metz #1075)	300.00+	700.00

Ref: Greentown Glass, The Indiana Tumbler and Goblet Company by James Measell.

1077
Grasshopper with Insect

1097
Tiny Lion

1100
Frolicking Bears

1090
Dragon

1013
Birds in Frame

1075
Squirrel

1823
Hand and Bar

1074
Squirrel Salt

1036
Flamingo

82

No. 1977 – GRASSHOPPER WITH INSECT – L.V.-38 – K. Bk. 1-88. Listed but not pictured in my first book, shown in my Booklet No. 2; I'm happy to be able to show a piece with the insect for it is now becoming scarce as the speculators are toying with it. If you get a chance to see a piece which is old you certainly will not be fooled by the *reproduction goblets* which are flooding the country. I've never seen an old Grasshopper goblet nor a tumbler, however, Mrs. Lee, listed a goblet. The set was made in many pieces; many such as footed sauces, footed plates do not have the hoppers. Creamers, sugars, etc. are made both ways. It's a clear non-flint of the early 80s. Covered butter $75.00; covered sugar $65.00; celery $45.00; open sugar $30.00; covered compote $100.00; goblet $45.00. *Goblet not original, repro, but still sought, occasionally found in amber, canary, or blue add 100%; without insect, less 40%. Aka Long Spear.*

No. 1097 – TINY LION – (Tiny lion is broken from top of jam jar in picture) – K. Bk. 2-35. Shown in my Booklet No. 4. Kamm calls this LION AND CABLE but as the other lion pattern has a cable edge this might lead to confusion. Non-flint, clear or clear and frosted of the early 80s, made in Ohio. Pitchers, too, have the tiny lions atop the handles. Again no tumbler nor goblet has been found. Spooner $30.00; open sugar $25.00; creamer $45.00; butter $45.00; celery $45.00; covered sugar $50.00; covered compote $75.00.

No. 1100 – FROLICKING BEARS – This altogether charming tumbler was never listed until it appeared in my Booklet No. 5. I believe it to be of the late 60s as the grape border is very like that of Grape Band of that time. A water pitcher has been reported but that is all. It would fit into many classifications of collections but I think the category of humor in Pattern Glass would best fit. Tumbler $85.00; water pitcher $125.00. *Also found in green carnival. Pitcher sold for $10,000.00; tumbler for $8,000.00. U.S. Glass c 1910.*

No. 1090 – DRAGON – L.V. 36 – Mil. Bk. 2-130 – shown in my Booklet No. 1. Clear, non-flint of the 70s, a very important, well designed, carefully made pattern, created at a time when the industry was about at its peak. Detail of dragon is especially fine; I predict when collectors realize how good it is, it will be even scarcer than it is now. Sauce dish $225.00; open sugar $850.00; spooner $1,200.00; creamer $1,500.00; covered sugar $2,000.00; covered butter $2,000.00; celery $1,500.00; goblet $1,800.00. *McKee Bros. c 1870s. Design patent #4419 Oct. 18, 1870.*

No. 1823 – HAND AND BAR – Previously unlisted. This should not be confused with the other Hand pattern which carries a geometric pattern covering all pieces, but which has a very similar finial. I've seen mustard jar $20.00; covered jam jar $35.00; covered sugar $40.00. *Bryce Bros. #90 1883, U.S. Glass c 1891.*

No. 1075 – SQUIRREL – K. Bk. 4-60 – Lee-100 shows this water pitcher with a group of the earlier Squirrel (1071 in my first book). This is a much later, clear, non-flint water pitcher, another of the novelty group made by the Greentown Glass Co. in Indiana in the 90s. Value $300.00 – 400.00. *Occasionally found in chocolate $700.00.*

No. 1074 – SQUIRREL SALT – Clear, non-flint of the late 70s, early 80s. Salt $45.00.

No. 1013 – BIRDS IN FRAME – Previously unlisted, clear, non-flint 10" plate of the 80s. I've seen one other plate of the same pattern and it had a fancier border as if it were a tray and these were service plates. I know not. Plate $25.00.

No. 1036 – FLAMINGO – Mil.-61. Shown in my Booklet No. 2. Splendidly made, clear, non-flint of the 70s. Goblet has many discs on the stem. Open sugar $25.00; spooner $40.00; creamer $45.00; covered butter $65.00; goblet $55.00. *Not Frosted Stork or Flamingo Habitat which do not have this one's distinctive squared shape.*

1082
Horseradish Mug

1081
Horsehead's Medallion

1087
Lion & Baboon

1025
Dog Covered Compote

1055
Two Owls Covered Compote

1030
Thrush and Apple Blossoms

1615
Parrot and Fan—Plus

1033
Chicken

No. 1082 – HORSERADISH MUG – Clear, non-flint novelty of the 80s. Value $50.00.

No. 1081 – HORSEHEADS MEDALLION – L.V.-20 and shown in my Booklet No. 2. clear, and a very few, rare pieces in milk white, non-flint of the early 70s. Until I visited Portland, Maine, and saw the collection of this and other Portland glass I did not believe this pattern to be made there for their glass was of excellent workmanship and the one piece of this pattern which I had seen was carelessly made. After being there I was convinced the piece I had seen was not a representative piece and that as claimed, Portland Glass Co. did make this pattern. The wreath around the horse's head is very similar to that around Grape and Festoon and another pattern which the same factory manufactured. Spooner $45.00; open sugar $25.00; open compote $35.00; celery $50.00; creamer $45.00; covered sugar $50.00; covered compote $85.00; in milk white add at least another 100%.

No. 1087 – LION AND BABOON – K. – Bk. 3-57. Celery shown. Non-flint in clear and clear and frosted, celery shown is latter. Probably of late 70s or early 80s after the success of the other Lion and other animal patterns. The creamer has the lion's head on edge of rectangular handle and one of these curious supposedly baboon heads under the spout. There should be a tumbler or goblet, but none to date. Spooner $50.00; open sugar $40.00; compote $95.00; creamer $55.00; covered sugar $75.00; covered butter $95.00; covered compote $100.00.

No. 1025 – DOG COVERED COMPOTE – L.-99 shows this in the tall compote; this one is in the Sandwich Museum. Clear, non-flint of the 70s. Low covered compote $195.000; tall covered compote $300.00.

No. 1055 – TWO OWLS COMPOTE – Another compote from the Sandwich Museum. These owls are somewhat like the birds on finial of Frosted Flower Band sugar. Clear, non-flint of the 70s; compote $300.00.

No. 1030 – THRUSH AND APPLE BLOSSOMS – Mil. Bk. 2-30. Clear, non-flint of the mid 80s. At present only goblet has been noted. Much sought by goblet collectors, goblet $150.00. *Aka Singing Birds. Northwood 1914.*

No. 1615 – PARROT AND FAN-PLUS – Had a collector told me he had seen this goblet I would have been sure he was mistaken; believe it or not, here is the picture and I have handled the goblet which belongs to Mr. Clarence Clawson. It is exactly the same as the well known Parrot and Fan only on *one panel only* there is a tiny bird pursuing a bee. Goblet $125.00.

No. 1033 – CHICKEN – L.V. 20. All clear and clear with frosted chicken finials, non-flint of the mid 70s. Altogether lovely. Open sugar $15.00; compote $20.00; creamer $35.00; covered butter $15.00; covered jam jar $75.00; covered sugar $55.00; covered compote $95.00. *Aka Frosted Chicken.*

1052
Flying Stork—Two Pieces; Jam Jar—Goblet

1048
Plain Swan

1037
Swan Mid Rushes

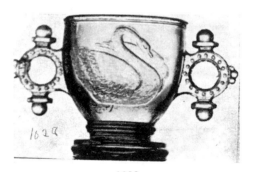

1028
Swan Mustard

1043
Panelled Swan

1039
Swan Mid Greenery
Two Views

No. 1052 – FLYING STORK – Mil. Bk. 2-117 and shown in by Booklet No. 6. Clear, non-flint of the 80s. Decor of three storks is done in same manner as in Cupid and Venus. Goblet $95.00.

No. 1052 – FLYING STORK JAM JAR – I believe this to be the jam jar of the pattern above and I show it here to warn novice collectors that a pattern may vary slightly as applied to different pieces. The cover is original; it was a stock cover pattern which I've found lately used on several patterns. Covered jam jar $50.00.

No. 1048 – PLAIN SWAN – Unlisted until shown in my Booklet No. 4. The pattern SWAN as we've found it before had this unit on a mesh background, otherwise they were the same. All swan patterns are scarce. Clear, non-flint of the 80s. Goblet $100.00; footed sauce $20.00; spooner $45.00; open sugar $30.00; covered butter $85.00; creamer $45.00; covered sugar $65.00. *Came in variety of colors including opaque pink, butterscotch, lavender and transparent colors. Design patent #12887, April 18, 1882, to D. Barker of the Brilliant Glass Co. He joined Canton Glass in 1883.*

No. 1037 – SWAN MID RUSHES – Clear, non-flint of the 80s; previously unlisted. From the collection of the Melvilles in Wisconsin. Design in the same structure as that of Cupid and Venus. Goblet $100.00.

No. 1043 – PANELLED SWAN – K. Bk. 5-127 calls it SWAN WITH TREE. If you confuse this with SITTING SWAN or SWIMMING SWAN in my first book I'd have you note the wings, which in this are uplifted while in the former they are not; also goblet does not have a ring in the middle of the stem. Non-flint of the 80s. Goblet $125.00; water pitcher $195.00.

No. 1028 – SWAN SUGAR – L. 127 – Clear, non-flint of the 80s. This originally had a cover, the finial of which was shaped like one of the handles. Covered sugar $45.00; sugar without cover $20.00; *mug $40.00. Atterbury. Uncommon in colors, amber +50%, canary +75%, and deep blue +100%.*

No. 1039 – SWAN MID GREENERY – K. Bk. 3-36 calls it simply SWAN but as there was a very well known early pattern by that name I've added to it. Two views give different sides which vary. Clear and milk white, non-flint of the 70s. Clear spooner (shown), open sugar $25.00; covered sugar $85.00; creamer $40.00; milk glass same value.

1132
Alligator

1115
Two Giraffes

1118
Two Camels

1129
Two Tigers

1158
Bear Climber

1086
Monkey Climber

1123
Etched Elephant

1127
Leopard

EARLY ETCHED GLASS

I use the term "early" here although it does not signify the early flints of the 30s or 40s; it is used, rather to distinguish this glass from that of the late 80s and 90s which was trimmed with a single band of fern or leaf etching. I know some of these were made in the late 60s but I've never been positive about locale of their manufacture, but now I've made up my mind they were made by the New England Glass Co. I have no proof of this, I've simply compared their etching on glass of the period with the product of this company and since I've started an intensive search for this glass, I've found a preponderance of it in Massachusetts. Some of the best art work in pattern glass is to be found in the designing of this glass; the goblets, which are the things most frequently found, afford endless variety of combinations. One Ohio collector has a zoo, another, a flower garden.

No. 1132 - ALLIGATOR – Clear, non-flint of the late 60s. Very scarce, and need I say, very desirable. I believe this is one of the many fine etched ones which belong to Mr. Clarence Clawson of Ohio. Goblet $200.00 – 300.00.

No. 1115 – TWO GIRAFFES – Another of the same family, evidently created by the same hand. Goblet $200.00 – 300.00.

No. 1118 – TWO CAMELS – Still another of the same family, work of the same artist and I mean artist in the true sense of the word. Goblet $200.00.

No. 1129 – TWO TIGERS – Another product of the same designer's hand belonging to the same family. Goblet $200.00.

No. 1158 – BEAR CLIMBER – This is the way the artist saw Mr. Bruin, who seems chagrined as if something had eluded him or as if he expected the tree to be taller. Goblet $200.00.

No. 1086 – MONKEY CLIMBER – This picture was sent to me by Mr. Kingsley of Portland, Oregon, and it is not as clear as we get. The artist had a genuine sense of humor. This is possibly the scarcest of the group, goblet $200.00 – 300.00.

No. 1123 – ETCHED ELEPHANT – Shown in my Booklet No. 3. Because he might become confused with the other elephant goblet, I've added, "etched." Note palm trees are the same as in others and the humor is there; probably is the same artist. Isn't he a playful beastie? Goblet $200.00.

No. 1127 – LEOPARD – Another matching one above, same shape and double knob stem, and artist displays power to give beast character, this time its fierceness. Goblet $200.00.

NOTE: In all of these goblets, etching appears only on one side. First six are the same graceful shape and have the same kind of stem. The last two are similar in shape.

1121
Stag

1114
Ibex

1106
Forest Fantasy Two Views

1180
Stork and Flowers

1093
Elk Medallion
Two Views

1044
Heron

90

No. 1121 – STAG – Another of the family of clear, non-flint etched goblets of the late 60s. Goblet same shape as two on preceding page. Not listed until shown in my Booklet No. 3. Same matchless design as the others, note the stance of this animal and see how it gives one the feeling of alertness. Goblet $75.00.

No. 1114 – IBEX – Another previously unlisted member of the same family. This goblet has the same shape as the six on preceding page; obviously these were the work of the same factory and the same talented designer. Goblet $75.00.

No. 1106 – FOREST FANTASY – Two views shown. This poetic title was given to this hitherto unlisted member of the family by Mr. Clarence Clawson, of Ohio, the owner. It is truly a fantasy; in the trees sit monkeys, cockatoos and owls with wiser expressions than I've ever seen. The flora and fauna are out of this world, truly fantastic. Goblet $75.00.

No. 1180 – STORK AND FLOWERS – Here is an unlisted one with the shape of the second group on the preceding page; this one is from the Sandwich Museum. It is mono-grammed. I believe that much of this glass has escaped listing previously because it is tricky to photograph successfully. Goblet $75.00.

No. 1093 – ELK MEDALLION – *Not etched* but decor applied as in Psyche and Cupid. Heretofore unlisted, scarce, non-flint, clear of the early 70s. Two views shown. Goblet $95.00; *compote $150.00.*

No. 1044 – HERON – *Not etched*, listed in my first book where creamer is shown. Decor same type as Psyche and Cupid, most attractive. This celery is especially pretty. Celery $115.00; *creamer $40.00; spooner $45.00. Aka Blue Heron.*

I'd greatly appreciate hearing of other pieces in these etched patterns and the two above.

1136
Oasis-Camel Caravan

1157

1157
Tropical Villa Goblets—Compote

1157

1135
Deer and Dog (2 views)

1112
Flamingo Habitat

No. 1136 – CAMEL CARAVAN – Mil. Bk. 2-75 – K. Bk. 8-1 calls it OASIS. Clear, non-flint of the 70s, listed in my first book, shown in my Booklet No. 3. Goblet $85.00.

No. 1157 – TROPICAL VILLA – Two views of goblet shown, also covered compote; of same family as one above. If you are puzzled in seeing the difference between the two, the building in this and the stem of the goblet are points of variance. Heretofore unlisted. Goblet $75.00; compote $135.00.

No. 1112 – FLAMINGO HABITAT – Another of this group of early etched goblets which was unlisted until I noted it in my Booklet No. 3. I've seen footed sauces $15.00; celery $45.00; goblets $65.00; and cheese dish $135.00. *Hobbs Brockunier Glass Co. 1880s. Cheese dish w/cover $150.00; butter $95.00; creamer $60.00; spooner $50.00; goblet $55.00; covered sugar $85.00; pitcher $225.00; open compote $45.00; covered compote $120.00; wine $35.00.*

No. 1135 – DEER AND DOG – This is the one of these patterns which is well known and that is possibly because it was listed years ago by Mrs. Lee. Because the pattern has been collected so long the goblet is very scarce and brings $95.00; the "u" shaped one will bring $115.00. I never knew why goblet collectors made such a fuss over this latter shape of the goblet but that is the case.

I'm convinced that all of these etched patterns were originally made in sets and the following price schedule will cover them all. Footed sauces $18.00; spooner $40.00; open sugar $40.00; open compote $45.00; creamer $45.00; covered butter $95.00; celery $60.00; covered sugar $95.00; covered compote $125.00; water pitcher $135.00.

No. 1160 – ETCHED HORSE – Not pictured. Yes, there was a Horse. One of the disappointments of this book was that I could not get the goblet and the photographer together. He is etched on only one side as most of them are and the foliage by his side is the same as that of Etched Stork 1124 or Stag 1121 which are the same as it was, double knob stem. Exceedingly rare, value $225.00.

1120
Etched Lily of
The Valley

1124
Etched Stork

1139
Etched Swan

1142
Feeding Swan

1711
Etched Guimpe

1705
Stately

1160
Wide Etched Band

1740
Sophia

No. 1120 – ETCHED LILY-OF-THE-VALLEY – Clear, non-flint of the late 60s; comes with knob stem, shown and with plain stem. For some unknown reason, more of these than of any other member of these early etched are found; I know not why, unless that these were more popular and more were made. Goblet, plain stem $45.00; knob stem $50.00.

No. 1124 – ETCHED STORK – Another of the fine animal etched goblets. I use the term "etched" in the name of this and in the one above because in both cases there is a pattern trimmed with the design unit molded in the glass, and called by a like name. Scarce goblet $85.00.

No. 1139 – ETCHED SWAN – Here is another of the same family in the animals; at first glance it is very easy to confuse this one with the one next to it; they seem identical, but they are not. The main difference is in the shading of the wings and the background greenery. Goblet $85.00.

No. 1142 – FEEDING SWAN – This goblet, clear, non-flint, is possibly a trifle later than the etched ones; here the decor is in the mold in the same manner as Cupid and Venus. It is every bit as scarce as the etched one, goblet $75.00.

No. 1711 – ETCHED GUIMPE – Unlisted until noted in my Booklet No. 6. Clear, non-flint of the 80s. Spooner $15.00; covered butter $35.00; creamer $25.00; covered sugar $35.00. There was in all probability a goblet. Crochet Band would harmonize with it.

No. 1705 – STATELY – Clear, non-flint of the early 80s; closely resembles MOSQUE, Mil. Bk. 2-161. These later etched patterns are found in abundance and lack the character of the early ones. This one has better form than most. Goblet $12.50.

No. 1160 – WIDE ETCHED BAND – Clear, non-flint of the mid 80s. This is the type most of us have found on grandma's top pantry shelf. They are abundant. Goblet $10.00.

No. 1740 – SOPHIA – 1880 – Clear, non-flint of the 1880s, shows that this type of etched was here then. Goblet $8.00.

Many simple etched patterns are found on different blanks with differing bowls, stems, and sizes. Those with simple etched fern leaves, vines, etc. while attractive, do not command prices much above $15.00.

1102
Dahlia

1103
Zinnia

1146
Nicotiana

1105
Etched Morning Glory

1126
Birds and Roses

1149
Garden Fruits

1177
Nestlings

1138
Etched Grape

No.1102 – DAHLIA – Non-flint of the late 60s. Here are the flower goblets of the same general family as the etched animals shown previously. Most of these, too, carry the etching on only one side. How these folks of long ago must have loved these simple garden flowers; they used them so frequently in designs. Goblet $35.00.

No. 1103 – ZINNIA – Same family of etched goblet as one above. This is very like the Dahlia, but I believe the larger, coarser leaf was an attempt to interpret the zinnia. It is a rough old fashioned flower which added much color to life. At present, it has obtained new status with the subtle shades and shapes of petals. Goblet $35.00.

No. 1146 – NICOTIANA – Another of this etched family of the late 60s. Again, I'm not certain that is what the flower is but they are star-like and have large leaves, so I'll let it go at that. None of the pictures do justice to the beauty of these goblets, which are especially charming; to a city apartment they would bring a breath of a country garden; in the country they would be right at home. Goblet $35.00.

No. 1105 – ETCHED MORNING GLORY – Because there is the early flint with the morning glory in the mold, I'm using the added word in the name. I've seen this in plain stem $20.00, and knob stem, pictured $35.00.

No. 1126 – BIRDS AND ROSES – Another altogether charming naturalistic scene, pleasant to see on one's dining table. This goblet belongs to Mr. Clarence Clawson of Ohio. Goblet $40.00.

No. 1149 – GARDEN FRUITS – And still another of the etched family. I believe this one is from the collection of the Willard Melvilles of Wisconsin. Goblet $35.00.

No. 1177 – NESTLINGS – I show this lovely one in my Booklet No. 5. I wish you might see the goblet. Mother and father bird stand near to the nest while three gaping mouths wait to be fed. Goblet $40.00.

No. 1138 – ETCHED GRAPE – This one is found more often than any of the others. Goblet $35.00; water pitcher, bulbous has been reported $75.00.

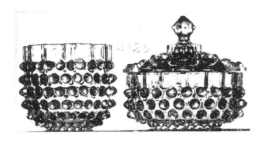

2113
Hob in Square

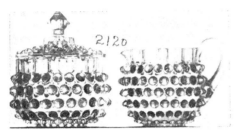

2120
Squat Ruffled Hob

2103
Sauce Plain Hobnail

1912
English Hobnail Condiment Set

2106
Hobnail With Scalloped Top

2111
Pointed Edge Hobnail

HOBNAIL

If you have a non-collecting husband who thinks all old glass is "junk," here's your bait. Many unsuspecting husbands have fallen to the lure of its sparkle. Any glass which acts its part well is good glass and hobnail does just that. There are many who do not have an acute sense of form and line and proportion but they like sparkle and gleam; the glass "with the little bumps" has just this and fills the bill perfectly, and yet it does not go to the length of the "cut glass." In this pattern the clear wins as much attention as the colored so Father's pocket book does not get too severe a wrench. I've seen many a good man captivated by it and go on to become a serious collector.

There are many qualities of Hobnail but so far I've only seen one piece in flint and that was when it was combined with thumbprint, No. 459 – HOBNAIL AND THUMB-NAIL in my first book now worth $75.00; in the earlier hobnails the points seem to be closer together and there are hobs on the bottom, except on erect pieces such as goblets.

No. 2120 – SQUAT RUFFLED EDGE HOBNAIL – K. Bk. 2-100 shows what she calls HOBNAIL WITH COL-ORED BAND and which she states is late and comes in frosted blue, clear and with colored bands. The latter part of the statement is correct but it is not a late hobnail pattern. I'm picturing a four piece set here in canary, all pieces of which have a ground pontil mark, which while not signifying blown glass, as I explain elsewhere, does mean comparative early manufacture, of glorious quality; the frosted blue is choice and very scarce; a clear with applied yellow band is most plentiful. Clear, spooner $30.00; open sugar $25.00; canary or with amber band an additional 100%; blue an additional 75%; frosted blue 100%; creamer $30.00; covered butter $50.00; for color same additional as for spooner. *Hobbs Brockunier #323 Dewdrop 1886. Amber band is called Frances ware. Also in cran-berry and light green add 150%.*

No. 2104 – PLAIN HOBNAIL – Shown in my fist book, this sauce now $10.00. *Columbia Glass, c 1890.*

No. 2113 – HOBNAIL IN SQUARE – K. Bk. 5-130. Clear, and frosted non-flint made in Ohio in 1887. Colors were also made. Large flat sauce $8.00; open sugar $25.00; spooner $30.00; covered butter $45.00; creamer $30.00; covered sugar $35.00. Frosted same value; canary 100% additional; amber 25% added; blue 75% additional. *Mug $35.00. Aetna Glass #335, 1887. Aka Hobnail in Diamond.*

No. 2106 – SCALLOPED TOP-THUMBPRINT BASE – Shown in my booklet No. 4. Clear, non-flint of the 80s, one of the better of the hobnail patterns. Valued under Plain Hobnail in my first book, but be certain and adjust prices as per suggestions given elsewhere.

No. 2111 – POINTED TOP (EDGE) HOBNAIL – This berry bowl and berry dish is one of the most attractive members of the family, sauce dish, now $15.00; bowl $45.00.

No. 1912 – ENGLISH HOBNAIL CONDIMENT SET – This is the original group of this very popular condiment set. Non-flint, clear, of the late 80s and really not a member of the Hobnail family. This set is from the collection of Mrs. Kenneth Wakefield of Massachusetts. Complete set $135.00.

2114
Hobnail in Big Diamond

2119
Hobnail with Curved Bars

2103
Child's Set Creamer

2110
Hobnail with
Thumbprint Base

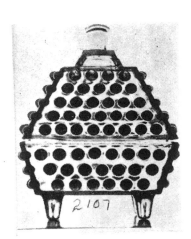

2107
Footed Square Hobnail

2104
Hobnail with Ornamented Band

2092
Panelled
Thousand Eye

2091
Banded Thousand
Salt Shaker

No. 2114 – HOBNAIL IN BIG DIAMOND – L.V. 66 calls it HOB WITH BARS although on pl. 74 she calls another pattern by the same name. Clear, non-flint made in Pennsylvania in the 80s in set although I believe no goblet has been found to date. Spooner $30.00; open sugar $25.00; creamer $35.00; covered butter $55.00; covered sugar $45.00. *Challinor & Taylor #307; U.S. Glass 1890s.*

No. 2148 – HOBNAIL IN DIAMOND – K. Bk. 4-64 (not pictured). Clear, non-flint, contemporary of the above which it resembles, same value as above. In this the lines forming the big diamond are covered with hobnail.

No. 2119 – HOBNAIL WITH CURVED BARS – L.V.–Where it is given the same name as 2114 above, although it is very different; in this two wide panels of six rows of hobnail are separated by two rows of horizontally curved bands. Clear, non-flint of the 80s. Prices would be those of Hob in Big Diamond. Tumbler $25.00; water pitcher $55.00; round water tray with matching pattern $40.00. Many water trays do not match in pattern, this one does. *Doyle/U.S. Glass 1890s.*

No. 2103 – CHILD'S SET CREAMER – There is a four piece set in the plain Hobnail in clear and colored; this creamer is 2½" tall and is amber. Toy sets are running very high; clear $150.00; canary $300.00; amber $250.00; blue $250.00. I've just added the blue one to my own collection. *Model Flint.*

No. 2107 – FOOTED SQUARE HOBNAIL – L.84 – One of the finest, rarest types of early hobnail and as scarce as hen's teeth. Square with little feet on each of four corners in clear, and colors and the colored opalescent which are exceptionally fine. Spooner $45.00; open sugar $35.00; celery $45.00; covered sugar $50.00; creamer $40.00; covered butter $55.00; canary additional 100%; amber additional 25%; blue additional 75%; colored opalescent canary additional 100%; amber additional 35%; blue additional 75%. *LaBelle Glass Co. c 1889.*

No. 2110 – HOBNAIL WITH THUMBPRINT BASE – Same quality and same values as Hobnail 2103 listed in my first book. *Salt and pepper found on glass stand with handle. Creamer and sugar reproduced in colors.*

No. 2092 – PANELLED THOUSAND EYE – Mil. Bk. 2-23 – K. Bk. 2-66. Clear, non-flint of the 80s, listed in my Booklet No. 1. I'm in doubt as to whether this is a true Thousand Eye because the distinguishing characteristic of the pattern is the tiny diamond between the eyes and here this is divided into four geometric figures. Makes a splendid pattern to use with Thousand Eye because in this, one does not have to worry about reproduction goblets. Goblets $40.00. *Aka Daisy Square. Richards & Hartley/U.S. Glass 1890s.*

No. 2091 – BANDED THOUSAND EYE-BANDED – A scarce type of the pattern. All I've ever seen is the shakers, though doubtless more was made. Clear shaker $40.00; canary 100% more; amber 30% more; blue 80% more; clear pair $85.00; same percentage increase for colors.

No. 2104 – HOBNAIL WITH ORNAMENTAL BAND – Aka Double Eye Hobnail. Found in clear, amber, blue. Spooner $30.00; mug $25.00; covered sugar $45.00. Colors 25% – 75% more.

2476
Shell and Jewel

2134
Ellipse and Fan

2032
Scroll & Dots

2132
Raindrop in Diamond

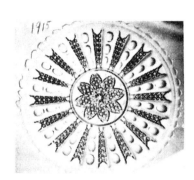

1915
English Hobnail and
Thumbprint

2183
Heavy   Jewel

2005
Enigma

No. 2476 – SHELL AND JEWEL – A rather poor picture was shown in my first book and in that there was a minor discrepancy between it and the pattern and the picture shown there. No small wonder for what I was picturing was the Canadian made pattern, which we American authors had claimed as ours and which is not; it was made in Canada. More on that elsewhere. Type shown in first book had shorter shell and a row of balls between the fans on the edge. *Originally a premium, relatively common. Tumbler $22.00; pitcher $45.00. Occasionally found in cobalt blue, with gold trim, 100% more.*

No. 1915 – ENGLISH HOBNAIL AND THUMBPRINT – L.14. Clear, non-flint of the 80s, no goblet nor tumbler yet found. Plates, 8", 10", shown $12.00 either; sauce dish $5.00; bowls $8.50; celery $20.00; spooner $15.00. Probably was more.

No. 2132 – RAINDROP IN DIAMOND – Unlisted until shown in my Booklet No. 4. Clear, non-flint of the late 80s. Lemonade glass shown $12.00. Let me hear of more, please.

No. 2134 – ELLIPSE AND FAN – Previously unlisted, clear, non-flint of the late 80s. Butter dish $40.00. Probably a set. *Aka Beaded Ellipse and Fan. U.S. Glass 1905.*

No. 2183 – HEAVY JEWEL – L.-37–K. Bk. 3-8484. Medium heavy, non-flint of the late 80s. Covered butter $35.00; open sugar $15.00; spooner $18.00; creamer $15.00; tumbler $15.00; covered sugar $25.00. *Fostoria #1225, c 1904.*

No. 2005 – ENIGMA – Mil. 140 – K. Bk. 2-49. Clear, non-flint of the 90s which Stanley Brothers states was made in Gas City, Indiana. Its original name was WYOMING. Spooner $40.00; open sugar $30.00; creamer $45.00; covered butter $65.00; covered sugar $50.00; goblet rare $265.00. *Preferred name: Wyoming. U.S. Glass #15081, c 1903. Cakestand $100.00; covered compote $130.00; syrup $225.00; wine $125.00.*

No. 2032 – SCROLL AND DOTS – Mil. 102 – K. Bk. 2-126 calls it SILVER SHEEN. Clear, non-flint of the early 80s. The background is composed of very fine concentric parallel, horizontal lines over which is a design of lines forming a diamond band circling the piece. Above this band and below it the lines form elongated loops; in the center of the diamonds are dots. Creamer $25.00; spooner $25.00; open sugar $20.00; covered butter $40.00; covered sugar $35.00. *Aka Maypole. McKee Bros. c 1901.*

1326
Dewdrop with Star

1324
Diamonds & Dewdrops

1316
Chain and Star Band

1302
Effulgent Star

1521
Twinkle Star

1671
Fan and Star

1323
Spooner
Star and Bars

1323
Plate

No. 1326 – DEWDROP WITH STAR – Made in many forms which are listed in my first book but where it is not pictured. The dish with large domed cover mentioned there should have been termed a "cheese dish." These are now $85.00. As there is no exact goblet to this pattern, one of the dewdrop patterns is a better choice than one of the star ones. *Many reproductions in salt dips, especially color. Campbell Jones and Co., c 1877.*

No. 1324 – DIAMONDS AND DEWDROPS – Mil. Bk. 2-68. Shown in my Booklet No. 5. Clear, non-flint of the 80s. Goblet $12.00.

No. 1316 – CHAIN AND STAR BAND – Mil. 23. Clear, non-flint of the early 70s, although a flint goblet has been reported. Goblet, non-flint $15.00; flint $35.00.

No. 1302 – EFFULGENT STAR – Mil. Bk. 2-122–STAR GALAXY–K. Bk. 8-78 may be this pattern, but the stem of the cakestand shown is not the same as this star and so I hesitate to put it in the same family as stems are a family characteristic. Clear, non-flint of the early 80s. Goblet $35.00; cakestand $65.00. *Central Glass #876 c 1880, U.S. Glass 1891.*

No. 1521 – TWINKLE STAR – Mil. 30 – K. Bk. 4-122 calls it FROST FLOWER as she shows it frosted. Clear, or clear and frosted, non-flint of the 80s. Goblet $25.00; creamer $30.00; water pitcher $55.00; an added 10% for frosting. Undoubtedly is a set. *Preferred name: Utah. Butter $45.00; spooner $35.00; covered sugar $40.00; cakestand $55.00; celery $55.00; covered compote $85.00; cruet $65.00; syrup $95.00; wine $25.00.*

No. 1671 – FAN AND STAR – L.V. 66 – Mil. Bk. 2-104 calls it ILEX. Clear, non-flint, made in Pennsylvania in the late 70s or early 80s, in many pieces. Flat sauce $5.00; bowls, open compotes, low foot, open sugar, spooner $15.00; tall open compote $25.00; celery $20.00; creamer $20.00; covered butter $35.00; covered sugar $25.00; jam jar $30.00; low covered compote $35.00; water pitcher $40.00; goblet $25.00. *Challinor & Taylor #304, c 1885, U.S. Glass 1891.*

No. 1323 – STAR AND BARS – Mil. 122 – Clear, non-flint of the late 70s or early 80s. I've seen a jam jar $35.00; goblet $25.00; and open sugar shown $15.00; and large plate which I'm quite certain belongs to this pattern $20.00. Frequently in trays, plates, cheese dishes, the pattern was elaborated, and most often the bread plate was made into a motto plate.

2530
Dewey Cruet

2180
Jewel & Dewdrop

2180
Jewel and Dewdrop

2178
Jewelled Pendants

2371
Shield

2129
Beaded Bull's Eye and Drape

2128
Beaded Raindrop

No. 2530 – DEWEY (preferred name) OR FLOWER FLANGE – K. Bk. 1-83 calls this FLOWER FLANGE and I prefer that name and so listed it in my first book but now under its title of Dewey it has become one of the stars of the Greentown galaxy at out of this world prices for a very ordinary clear, and colored non-flint glass of the late 90s, made at Greentown, Indiana. Shown is the cruet in amber with the original stopper which would bring at least $175.00. Indiana Glass (Dunkirk) 1911. Can be found in clear, amber, canary, emerald green and some pieces rarely in cobalt, opaque white, Nile green, chocolate. Cruet: clear $165.00; amber $175.00; canary $190.00; emerald green $175.00; Nile green $1,250.00; chocolate $2,000.00.

No. 2180 – JEWEL AND DEWDROP – L. 75 – Mil. 47 – K. Bk. 1-77. Shown in my Booklet No. 2. Clear, non-flint of the 90s, came out under the name of KANSAS. The goblets and mugs came in two qualities, a dull, non-clear, and a bright clear type, both non-flint. One has to be very careful of these clear goblets and mugs because most of them are Kokomo Glass. The bread tray which I show here is an unusually attractive piece and no fake has been seen in that yet. Grayed goblet $15.00; mug, same $10.00; all clear goblet $85.00; mug $65.00; bread tray $75.00; wine $85.00; cakestand, 8", 9", 12" $30.00, $35.00, 48.00; open compotes, 6", 8", 9" $75.00, $100.00, $120.00; any size open bowl $40.00; scarce spooner $65.00; flat sauce $15.00; relish dish $25.00; toothpick $65.00; salt shaker $55.00; creamer $75.00; covered butter $100.00; covered sugar $85.00; syrup $225.00; milk pitcher $125.00; water pitcher $75.00. *Preferred name now: KANSAS. U.S. Glass #15072, c 1901, Kokomo Glass #8 c 1914. Rose stain 250%+.*

No. 2178 – JEWELLED PENDANTS – Mil. Bk. 2-133. Clear, non-flint of the 80s. Goblet $12.00. Should be more. *Columbia Glass #23, c 1887, U.S. Glass 1891.*

No. 2371 – SHIELD – K. Bk. 4-147 shows this stating she thinks it is not American. I'm quite certain it is American, clear, non-flint of the late 80s. Pitcher $10.00. *English.*

No. 2129 – BEADED BULL'S EYE AND DRAPE – K. Bk. 1-80. Clear, non-flint of the late 80s. Comes in child's size. Either size pitcher $10.00. *Highly sought after by preferred name: ALABAMA. Found in full range of pieces. Butter $125.00; cakestand $150.00; celery vase $75.00; cruet $110.00; creamer (table) $55.00, (individual) $65.00; spooner $55.00; pitcher $95.00; syrup $175.00; compote $95.00; toothpick $75.00. Occasionally found with ruby stain 300% more; emerald green 150% more.*

No. 2128 – BEADED RAINDROP – K. Bk. 3-108. Clear, non-flint of the late 80s or early 90s. *Creamer only known, $10.00; U.S. Glass #20036, c 1915.*

A FINE PLACE TO SEE GOOD GLASS

I've listed elsewhere here many museums with fine glass collections for you to see; but one must see it more than once. A fine show is an excellent place. When a show advertises, "Something for Everybody–Articles from $1.00 to $10,000.00," I'm down right suspicious. When you see a show which advertises and boasts mainly of the number of exhibitors, you can be equally wary. When you enter a show and see displays of costume jewelry, and twenty-five year old embroidery towels and centerpieces, you had better watch out; it is apt to be one which sends its prospectus to resale dealers throughout the land. The right type of show is careful of the type of dealer it invites to participate. At times a good show may have a good dealer go sour, or may err. If you see the wrong kind of merchandise in the right kind of show, I'm sure the management would appreciate a report, at the office, immediately. When you do this, you are helping honest dealers, novice collectors and the antique world as a whole.

2087
Crackle Glass

2068
Orange Peel Band

1942
Strippled Bar

528
Cleat

1952
Arched Fans

2501
Hexagon Block

1549
Daisy Whorl with
Diamond Band

1750
Pentagon

No. 2087 – CRACKLE GLASS – Mil. 31–Clear and colored glass of the 80s. This pitcher has a ground pontil, but as I explain elsewhere a pontil mark is not always a mark of a blown piece. It is a mark of comparatively early manufacture, as is this applied handle. The pitcher shown here is clear but the texture gives it a lovely frosty appearance. Made in sets; and not too plentiful; clear: wine, goblet $85.00; creamer $75.00; water pitcher $120.00; various shades of canary 100% additional; varying shades of amber 25% additional, many shades of blue 50% additional, ruby, rose and other shades of red 100% additional. Not EAPG, *Elegant Depression*.

No. 2068 – ORANGE PEEL BAND – Mil. Bk. 2-94. Shown in my Booklet No. 6. In my first book, I stated I thought his was the same as Stippled Bowl. It is not. This differs greatly in texture, being like the roughest orange skin you ever touched, very intriguing. Clear, non-flint of the early 80s and a very suitable goblet to use where the feeling of strength is desired, such as with a setting of Ironstone or scenic Staffordshire china. Wine, goblet $25.00. *Occasionally found in flint.*

No. 1942 – STIPPLED BAR – L.V. 63. Clear and stippled or colored and stippled, non-flint of the 80s. I've seen it with bars in the red and bars in the amber besides the all clear. Clear spooner $35.00; open sugar $20.00; 7" plate $15.00; tumbler $20.00; creamer $25.00; covered butter, unusual pagoda shape cover, covered sugar $35.00; with amber stripe an additional 30%; with red an additional 100%. *U.S. Glass #15044, c 1895.*

No. 528 – CLEAT – Heretofore unlisted but known by this name and the only piece in this pattern which has appeared. Clear, non-flint, evidently dates from the 50s, there must be more. The pitcher is most unusual with large, heavy prisms extending far out from the body of the piece. Handle is applied. Pontil shape is different. Water or milk pitcher $200.00; *decanter $150.00; lantern $250.00.*

No. 1952 – ARCHED FANS – Previously unlisted, clear, late, of the 90s, but very attractive goblet, in combination of clear and frosted shown here. *This is CAPRICE by Cambridge Glass, 1940 – 1957. Not EAPG.*

No. 2501 – HEXAGON BLOCK – Mil. Bk. 2-50 – K. Bk. 1-111. Clear, non-flint of the 90s. In speaking of this pattern, Mrs. Kamm mentions resonance, which might lead to a misunderstanding as it has no ring being lime glass. Goblet $40.00; *pitcher $75.00; spooner $35.00. Dalzell Gilmore & Leighton, c 1895.*

No. 1549 – DAISY WHORL – K. Bk. 4-8 – Mil. Bk. 2-121 pictures the spooner in this and calls it DAISY WHORL WITH DIAMOND BAND and in Mil. Bk. 1-58, he calls the same pattern COUCHMAN. Here he shows the goblet. Non-flint of the late 70s; comes in sets and in colors; spooner $30.00; open sugar $15.00; covered butter $45.00; open compote $20.00; covered sugar $25.00; covered compote $35.00. *Color 50% more.*

No. 1750 – PENTAGON – K. Bk. 3-101. Clear, non-flint of the 80s. All I've heard of is the individual creamer $15.00; tankard type water pitcher $65.00. *George Duncan & Son, c 1888.*

2296
Beaded Swirl

2297
Beaded Swirl with
Disc Band

2290
Cyclone

2293
Bar & Swirl

2275
Nokomis Swirl

1925 — Pebbled Swirl

Sauce

No. 2296 BEADED SWIRL – Shown also in my Booklet No. 4 where I mention a deep green; prices for this spooner, open sugar $20.00; finger bowl, flat relish $12.00; tumbler, $15.00; butter, $35.00; creamer $25.00; goblet, covered sugar $25.00. It used to be that the scarce light green was the expensive color and I believe it still is among seasoned collectors but this dark green seems to have won the popularity contests. Some prefer it with all of the gilt shiny and bright, most decorators want just a hint of it left, I prefer it all removed. There are those who flourish under bright sunlight, I prefer the mist of morning or eventide where defects don't blaze forth as they do under the light of a blistering sun. To each his own. *George Duncan & Sons, c 1890. U.S. Glass c 1891.*

No. 2297 – BEADED SWIRL WITH DISC BAND – Listed in my book and also shown in Booklet No. 4. Besides the clear and green this contemporary of Beaded Swirl above comes in most fascinating combinations with amber where the discs are colored in it or other colors. Same values as colored. *U.S. Glass #15085, c 1904.*

No. 2290 – CYCLONE – 2297 – Listed in my Booklet No. 6. Clear, non-flint of the 80s – Mil. 45. Should be in colors also but to date, none have been reported. Clear: goblet $25.00; open sugar $10.00; spooner $20.00; celery $22.00; creamer $15.00; covered butter $30.00; covered sugar $25.00; tumbler $15.00.

No. 2293 – BAR AND SWIRL – Mil. Bk. 2-79. Shown in my Booklet No. 6. Clear, non-flint of the 80s with a most interesting stem. A setting made of two of these goblets two Cyclone and two of the following one would be much more attractive than one of goblets all of one pattern; too would be easier to locate. Same values as Bar and Swirl or Cyclone. *Central Glass #884, c 1880s. U.S. Glass, c 1890s.*

No. 2275 – NOKOMIS SWIRL – Mil. 91. Shown in my Booklet No. 6. Another of the swirl family. Contemporary of the others; this one has been found in canary, amber, light green, blue. Clear priced same as clear Cyclone; for colors add canary, light green 100% additional; amber 30% additional; blue 75% additional with exception of goblets which run as follows: canary or green $35.00; amber $22.00; blue $30.00.

No. 1925 – PEBBLED SWIRL – Mil. Bk. 2-20. Clear and heavily stippled glass of the 80s. Most attractive goblet shown $25.00; flat sauce, shown $7.00; open sugar $10.00; spooner $20.00; creamer $20.00; covered sugar $25.00.

1564
Fishscale Swirl

2285
Double Line Swirl

2289
Thumb. & Pan. Swirl
or Swirl & Dot

1928
Diagonal Frosted Ribbon

2053
Beaded Ovals

1990
Jacob's Coat

1370
Buckle Compote

No. 1564 – FISHSCALE SWIRL – Mil. Bk. 2-51. A most interesting, clear, non-flint of the late 1890s. This pattern seems more closely related to the Fishscale pattern family than to the Swirl family in weight and shape of goblets. It is slightly earlier than most of the swirls. Goblet $45.00; spooner $30.00; open sugar $25.00; creamer $30.00; covered butter $65.00; covered sugar $45.00. *Dalzell Gilmore & Leighton, c 1895.*

No. 2285 – DOUBLE LINE SWIRL – Mil. Bk. 2-20. Shown in my Booklet No. 1. Another most attractive member of the Swirl family and one which when seen in a setting is most pleasing; the unusual stem adds no little interest. Contemporary of Fishscale Swirl above and of same values.

No. 2289 – THUMBPRINT AND PANELLED SWIRL – Mil. 146 – SWIRL AND DOT – L.V.-63. Shown in my Booklet No. 6. Clear, non-flint of the late 80s, many of the pieces being of a very strange form. Seldom seen today and as some folks think queerness means great value and the mark of a real antique I've seen these pieces marked ridiculously high. Goblet, best looking piece $35.00; spooner $25.00; open sugar $25.00; covered dish $45.00; covered butter $65.00; celery $35.00; syrup $65.00; cruet $40.00; pair of salt shakers $55.00; covered sugar $45.00; water pitcher $65.00; all glass castor set, three bottles, $75.00; tumbler $30.00. *Central Glass #999, c 1891.*

No. 1928 – DIAGONAL FROSTED RIBBON – Mil. Bk. 2-23. Clear, non-flint of the early 80s. Rows of frosted alternate with rows of clear, diagonally around the pieces to make a pleasing whole. Goblet $40.00; spooner $30.00; open sugar $20.00; creamer $25.00; covered butter $50.00; covered sugar $40.00.

No. 2053 – BEADED OVALS – M.-47 – L.V.-30 shows what I believe to be the pattern with the ovals clear. My first book listed goblet only as then I had not seen other pieces. Spooner $20.00; open sugar $15.00; celery $20.00; covered butter $35.00; creamer $25.00; covered sugar $35.00; goblet $30.00.

No. 1990 – JACOB'S COAT – L.-115. Clear and amber, non-flint of the 80s. It's one pattern in which I've seen as much of the amber as I've seen of the clear. One does not see much of it; there is not much interest in the pattern with the fantastic name. Clear sauce $8.00; spooner $20.00; open sugar $12.00; covered butter $25.00; covered sugar $25.00; celery $20.00; amber 25% more.

No. 1370 – BUCKLE – Pattern is listed in my first book but I wanted to show the finial of the compote. Note how acorn is used vertically. From Sandwich Museum.

1370
Buckle Open Sugar

1376
Diamond Rosettes

1493
Short Tidy

1494
Long Tidy

534
Cuttle Bone

2266
English Hob Cross
or Klondyke

1461
Crossed Cords and Prisms Sauce

No. 1370 – BUCKLE – Listed in my first book and compote with interesting erect acorn finial shown on preceding page. Shown here for comparison with pattern next to it, Diamond Rosettes. *Attributed to Gillinder, Boston & Sandwich, and Union Glass.*

No. 1376 – DIAMOND ROSETTES – When my first book was published I had letters from folks who could not see the difference between these two patterns; then I did not have a like piece, now I have two open sugars and the difference is very marked. The rosette in the second pattern is no buckle, it has more rows of teeth and is placed lower on the bowl which leaves no room for the rays.

No. 1493 – SHORT TIDY-STAYMAN – Mil. Bk. 2-68. Clear, non-flint of the 80s. Same values as one below. *McKee Bros,. c 1880.*

No. 1494 – LONG TIDY-DRAPERY VARIANT – L.V.- 22 uses the latter name, I never use the term "variant" because it's been abused too much. Contemporary of above. Spooner, open sugar $8.00; bowls $8.00; egg cup $9.00; covered butter $15.00; covered sugar $15.00; goblet $35.00; creamer $10.00. *McKee Bros,. c 1880. OMN: Rustic.*

NO. 534 – CUTTLE BONE – Mil. Bk. 2-42. A clear, crisp, non-flint of the 80s. Goblet $25.00.

No. 2266 – ENGLISH HOBNAIL CROSS-KLONDYKE – K. Bk. 2-100. Put out at one factory under the trade mane of AMBERETTE. Non-flint, clear or frosted with color, the most popular being the frosted with cross in amber. Goblet $650.00; tumbler $225.00; covered sugar $325.00; covered butter $600.00; syrup $750.00; wine $600.00; water pitcher $1,200.00; cruet with original stopper $1,200.00. *Clear 125% less. Klondike. Dalzell, Gilmore & Leighton #75 & 75D. OMN: Amberette, c 1898.*

No. 1461 – CROSSED CORDS AND PRISM – Clear and colored of the 70s, amber sauce shown. This is a most intriguing pattern. I saw the milk glass spooner in it in the Sandwich Museum; the Bennington Museum has a clear spooner in it, so there was a set. Footed sauce, clear $8.00; spooner $20.00; milk glass, amber an added 50%.

AN EXPLANATION - NOT AN APOLOGY

As I read proofs I'm startled by the intimate character of these articles and by the number of "I's" they contain and I pause and wonder — is it scientific? "Rats!" says common sense. Pattern glass is the story of a product intimately connected with the lives of real people and it had to be told in that way. Let the presses roll!

1458
Draped Window

1215
Oriental Fan

1091
Gargayle

1632
Bone Stem

2529
Crescent and Fan

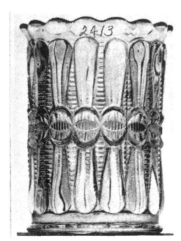

2605
Zenith Block

2413
Bow Tie

1437
Shield and Spike

1741
Prism and
Diamond Bars

No. 1458 – DRAPED WINDOW – Mil. Bk. 2-158; also shown in my Booklet No. 6. A carefully made fancifully designed, non-flint of the early 80s. The detail which went into the making of this mold was an expert piece of work; one can almost feel the texture of the curtain material. There are several goblets on this page which might lend themselves to another collection, "Fanciful Glass." goblet $12.00.

No. 1091 – GARGOYLE – Mil. Bk. 2-130. Clear, non-flint of the early 80s. Another unusual design resulting from a flight of fancy. Goblet $150.00. *Bellaire Goblet, 1886. U.S. Glass, 1891.*

No. 1215 – ORIENTAL FAN – Mil. Bk. 2-51. Another of the same imaginative type in non-flint clear glass of the 80s. This one is slightly more realistic. Goblet $35.00.

No. 1632 – BONE STEM – Heretofore unlisted, clear, non-flint, and to say the least, unusual goblets of the early 80s. Three bones, crossed, form the stem. The goblet is in the collection of the Willard Melvilles of Wisconsin. Goblet $75.00. Can you imagine what conversation pieces a group of goblets like these would make on a table? *Cobalt add 150%. King & Son $500, c 1890. U.S. Glass, 1891.*

No. 2529 – CRESCENT AND FAN – Mil. Bk. 2-128. Clear, non-flint, not fanciful, just bold as it is of the late 80s or early 90s and begins to reflect the gaudiness of the imitation cut glass of the period. It begins to lose the flavor of old glass. Goblet $30.00. *Aka Starred Scroll.*

No. 2615 – ZENITH BLOCK – Mil. Bk. 2-71. Clear non-flint of the 90s. Not bad in design, but not the mood of old glass. Goblet $22.00.

No. 2413 – BOW TIE – Mil. Bk. 2-5. Clear, rather heavy, non-flint of the mid 80s. In some of the pieces, namely the goblet and cakestand, the pattern is quite effective. Made in many pieces. Spooner $15.00; open sugar $10.00; bowls $15.00; creamer $20.00; covered butter $35.00; celery $25.00; large cakestand, covered sugar $35.00; goblet $85.00. *Thompson Glass #18, c 1889.*

No. 1437 – SHIELD AND SPIKE – Mil. Bk. 2-22. Clear, non-flint of the 80s. Goblet $25.00.

No. 1741 – PRISM AND DIAMOND BARS – Mil. 31. Clear, non-flint of the 80s. $25.00.

WHAT IS GOOD GLASS?

No one kind of glass has a monopoly on all good points. With some it's material, some it's age, some it's historical association, some it's scarcity, some it's beauty of line, some it's humor, some it's family association. Whatever it is, good glass is for you, that which fills its place the best and suits the size of your pocketbook, for "Any part that is acted well, is just as good as another." Find first what part you want your glass to play, you know your purse. Study first. Shop next.

2725
Watchman's
Lantern

1535
Tree of Life Epergne

1539
Infant Samuel

1188
Girl with Goose

2726
Portland Ewer

236
Frosted Leaf

236
Frosted Leaf Lamp

237
Oval Eye Frosted Leaf

PORTLAND GLASS

When one sees the rush for any piece of glass, no matter how late, how poorly designed or how cheaply it is made, and who sees people willing to pay an outlandish price for the piece just because it is classed as "Indiana Glass or Iowa Glass" one wonders at the taste and the wisdom of some collectors and the dealers and authors who promote such collecting philosophy. I admire and see the value of HOLLY AMBER, HORSE, CAT AND RABBIT OR JUMBO goblet or "BE VIRTUOUS" plate but I can't see that fine glass lends a special aura to other mediocre ware produced by the same or other factories in the same state. In the meantime some fine, well made and well designed patterns are ignored. One such pattern is TREE OF LIFE, made by the Portland Glass Co.

The Portland Glass Co. was a large firm, operating in the city of that name in Maine from 1864 until 1873. It produced many of our finest patterns in quantity. Dahlia in clear and colored, Jacob's Ladder, Classic, Frosted Ribbon, etc. In 1865, the factory shipped a twenty-five thousand dollar order of Dahlia to Indiana. Considering the price of glass then, that must have been a huge order. Miss Florence Dana, a niece of Mr. Frank H. Swan, who wrote the two books which are the texts on this glass, let us picture many pieces from her splendid collection and then took us to the Portland Art Museum, where we found more treasures to photograph. Miss Dana has continued the study of this factory and its products, and I feel she knows more about it than anyone else.

No. 2725 – WATCHMAN'S LANTERN – Mr. Swan found this lantern in a second hand store and found from the books of the Portland Glass Co. that C.P. Drackett was the watchman of the plant. The company also made these lamp shades for sale. *Blown globe.*

No. 1535 – TREE OF LIFE EPERGNE – From Portland Art Museum. Clear, non-flint, Tree of Life with red serpent twining around vase and the base. A one-of-a-kind piece; tradition says this was a special order, made for the governor's wife. *Also made by Boston & Sandwich and in England. #1535 is probably British because the scallops are flat on top and gilded as are other forms in England. American pieces are usually rounded and not painted gold.*

No. 1539 – INFANT SAMUEL EPERGNE – Another Tree of Life epergne, this one was the infant Samuel. Portland Art Museam. Value $450.00, *compote $250.00, candlestick $175.00, frosted 25% more. Hobbs, Brockunier.*

No. 1188 – GIRL WITH GOOSE – Hitherto unlisted. I believe this was made at Portland; matched by one with a little boy. Either non-flint of the 70s, clear, value $250.00.

No. 2726 – PORTLAND EWER – Ruby and clear, non-flint glass ewer of the 70s from Portland Art Museum. Really art glass. Value $200.00. *Blown $650.00.*

No. 236 – FROSTED LEAF – Shown in my first book but this lamp is so rare, I wanted my readers to see it. Kerosene lamp of late 60s or early 70s, base of black glass, bowl rare flint Frosted Leaf pattern. Lamp $500.00. I've had some queries about the creamer in this pattern in that the two leaves next to handles are not frosted. I've never found a pattern in which they were, I don't know why. Tumbler, $175.00.

No. 237 – OVAL EYE FROSTED LEAF – Hitherto unlisted, rare, clear flint relative of Frosted Leaf. Of late 60s, goblet $190.00.

1535
Goblets—Portland
1537
Sandwich Tree of Life Goblet

1536
Tree of Life
with Shield

1535
Handled Lemonade

1535
Bowl

1535
Salt

1535
Egg Cup

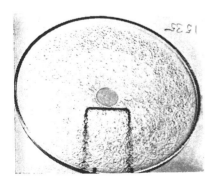

1535
Large Plate

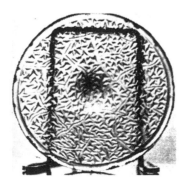

1535
Furniture Inset

1535
Sauce

120

No. 1535 – PORTLAND TREE OF LIFE GOBLET – Value $95.00; signed $175.00.

No. 1537 – SANDWICH TREE OF LIFE GOBLET – Value $95.00. Circa 1880s.

No. 1536 – PORTLAND TREE OF LIFE WITH SHIELD GOBLET – Value $295.00. Shown in my Booklet No. 5.

No. 1535 – PORTLAND TREE OF LIFE HANDLED LEMONADE – Value $100.00. Scarce *There is a pitcher in a frame with a hook for this cup $500.00 complete. 100% more for amethyst (not sun colored)*

No. 1535 – PORTLAND TREE OF LIFE FOOTED SAUCE – Value $25.00.

No. 1535 – PORTLAND TREE OF LIFE EGG CUP – Value $90.00. Scarce.

No. 1535 – PORTLAND TREE OF LIFE LOG SALT – Value $150.00. Rare.

No. 1535 – PORTLAND TREE OF LIFE LARGE PLATE – Value $40.00. This piece in the Sandwich Museum, the others are in the Portland Art Museum or in Miss Dana's collection.

No. 1535 – PORTLAND TREE OF LIFE GLASS INSETS FOR FURNITURE – In Europe, porcelain inserts were used to decorate furniture, but this is the only time I've heard of colored glass inserts being used here. These are 5" in diameter and come in canary, amber, blue and green, in differing shades and red. Values, clear $5.00; canary $7.00; amber $8.00; green $8.00; blue $10.00; ruby $12.00. *Also seen in clear Tree of Life coasters for furniture legs.*

Tree of Life can be found in amber, blue (shades vary), apple green, cranberry. Colors 100% – 200% more. Some pieces will have the name "Davis" intertwined in the pattern, presumably the mold designer. There can be confusion between Tree of Life and Overshot. The first has the pattern molded in and the latter is blown, then rolled in crushed glass "shot" giving it a much rougher texture.

TOO PARTICULAR?

Some people read the warnings and become uneasy. There are frequently those who are ever ready to add to that uneasiness with no basis for their criticism or at time a sinister motive. I know a collector of Three Face who became worried about his glass. Three Face has been reproduced three or four times but can still be caught by a practiced eye. A dealer who sells reproductions and who claims hers were made from the original molds said she could see no differences between his old and hers. She was selling reproductions. I have the booklet which the present Mrs. Duncan of the Duncan-Miller factory which produced the Three Face and for which Mrs. Miller was the model. This booklet specifically states that the mold of Three Face was lost in a fire which destroyed the factory. Something tells me the lady had an ulterior motive. An interesting side light here on the pattern Three Face — for one time some called it the Three Graces — there was controversy over who was the model. The factory settled it. A reader of mine, a neighbor of the present Mrs. Duncan suggested she send me a booklet. I learned much from it.

1535
Creamer

1535
Covered Sugar

1535
Lemonade

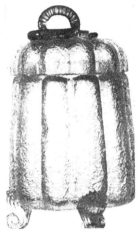

1535
Cracker Jar

1535
Celery

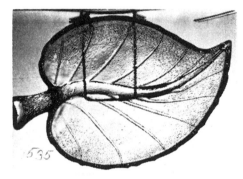

1535
Birch Leaf Sauce

1535
Creamer—Plated Holder

1535
Creamer

No. 1535 – PORTLAND TREE OF LIFE CREAMERS – Note the difference in handles between this one and the one below. Value $75.00.

No. 1535 – PORTLAND TREE OF LIFE CELERY – Value $75.00.

No. 1535 – PORTLAND TREE OF LIFE LEMONADE – Value $40.00.

OVERSHOT with applied handle and feet. Rare. Value $300.00.

No. 1535 – PORTLAND TREE OF LIFE COVERED SUGAR – Value $80.00.

No. 1535 – PORTLAND TREE OF LIFE CREAMER IN PLATED HOLDER – This comes in four piece set. $100.00 – 125.00.

No. 1535 – PORTLAND BIRCH LEAF SAUCE – Value $25.00. On this page also glass shown from Miss Dana or the Portland Art Museum.

REPRODUCTION BUGABOO

When all sees all that has been written on reproductions and hears all of the warnings, he may begin to wonder if collecting old glass, or in fact, any antique, is a profitable pastime. The fact that all of the warnings are issued means that the market is well policed and there is no reason for anyone being victimized. The care is needed, that is needed in doing any buying from a porkchop to a diamond ring. There are charlatans in all lines of business; you buy meat from a trusted butcher; if you were to buy a diamond, you would go to a trusted diamond merchant, you would not go out in the "sticks" searching for bargains. Why are these tactics considered fun in antique collecting? I know not. They may be fun, but of a costly variety.

Why collect a thing of which there are so many reproductions? If antiques had no value they would not be reproduced. The diamond, one of our most costly gems is most frequently reproduced. When reproductions stop, then we should worry.

There are those who think legislation to have all modern glass marked with date would solve the riddle. Would it? Think of the millions of pieces now on the market which would be legitimized because they are undated. No easy solution to many of our little problems, I fear.

1524
Tape Measure or
Shields

839
Lotus with Serpent

2227
Portland Cracker Jar

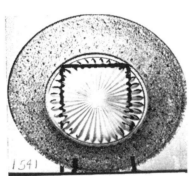

1541
Snowdrop or Ashland

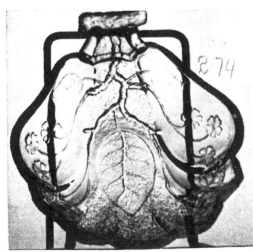

274
Derigo Pear

1542
Rose Band Sauce

1542
Rose Band

No. 1524 – TAPE MEASURE – K. Bk. 5-9 – Mil.-146 calls it SHIELDS. A product of the Portland Glass Co., clear, non-flint of the early 70s. Pitchers have applied handles. Flat sauce $10.00; goblet $30.00 (these two pieces shown are from the Portland Art Museum); covered sugar $50.00; butter $65.00; water pitcher $85.00.

No. 839 – LOTUS WITH SERPENT – Preferred GARDEN OF EDEN – Shown in my first book, but I wanted to show you this fine creamer $55.00; and spooner $40.00; from the Portland Art Museum.

No. 2227 – PORTLAND – I listed this in my first book, but I did not know of this cracker jar which is in the Portland Museum as the pattern was made at Portland. There were such huge quantities of this pattern in the midwest that I believe the pattern was reissued later at some midwest factory also. I recommended this as a simple pattern, inexpensive and easy to find and now it has fast become much scarcer. Many have collected sets for use. Prices have advanced somewhat as would be expected under a run. *This cracker jar would appear to be Fostoria's Long Buttress rather than Portland.*

No. 1541 – SNOWDROP – ASHLAND – Mil. Bk. 2-31 gives it this latter title but anyone who has handled it prefers the former. It is very lovely with its little drops on deeply stippled surface. I've seen a deep rectangular ice cream tray, similar to the one in Tree of Life and Leaf sauce dishes in the pattern which is shown in my first book. This large plate is from the Sandwich Museum. Large plate $30.00.

No. 1542 – ROSE BAND – Clear, non-flint of the early 70s, made by the Portland Glass Co. These two pieces are from the Portland Museum. Flat sauce $6.00; goblet $18.00. *Appears to be of later vintage, possibly 1920s, not Portland.*

No. 274 – DIRIGO PEAR – A fancy leaf sauce from the Portland factory. Clear, non-flint of the early 70s. From Miss Dana's collection. Sauce $30.00.

ANOTHER COMMON ERROR

I've heard a lecturer on pattern glass tell an audience to tap a glass and if it did not ring it was not good glass. That was unfortunate. At present, good glass in flint is scarce but a fine flint Ashburton goblet will not bring nearly the price of a Pigs in Corn or a Jumbo goblet. It is no measuring stick at all. There is no quick road to value or knowledge in this business. What make value? Demand and its resulting scarcity makes price which is not always true value, but if a piece is worth what one can get for it one must consider how long he will have it and for what he wants it. Quality pays in the long run, but quality of design is as important as quality of material. In a pattern of which there is a flint and a lime one, the lime one has very little value as compared to the flint. If your shop is in Indiana, the glass products of that state are very valuable to you if you are a dealer. I fear they would not be as popular on the eastern seaboard.

1335
Ribbon Band
with Pendants

2168
Dots & Dashes

1333
Dewdrop Drapery

1404
Pan. Diamonds &
Rosettes

2054
Beaded Circle

2054
Beaded Circle Celery

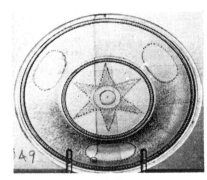

2049
Beaded Mirror Plate

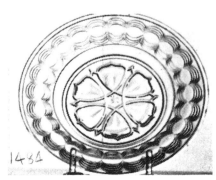

1484
Scalloped Lines Plates

No. 1335 – RIBBON BAND WITH PENDANTS – Mil. Bk. 2-60. Shown in my Booklet No. 5. Clear, non-flint of the 80s in a very whimsical pattern. Goblet $150.00. *Trenton Glass, Nova Scotia. OMN: Kenlee.*

No. 2168 – DOTS AND DASHES – Mil. Bk. 2-123. Shown in my booklet No. 5. Clear, non-flint of the 80s. Goblet $20.00.

No. 1333 – DEWDROP DRAPERY – Mil. Bk. 2-80. Shown in my Booklet No. 5. Clear, non-flint of the 80s. Goblet $45.00.

NO. 1404 – PANELLED DIAMONDS AND ROSETTES – Mil. Bk. 2-61. Shown in my Booklet No. 5. Clear, non-flint of the 80s. This goblet and the three above are all about the same weight and contour and make a most interesting combination. Why does one try to bother with so many patterns which are reproduced when a little searching among dealers who handle glass will bring forth things like these which are not reproduced? $25.00.

No. 2054 – BEADED CIRCLE – L.V.34 – Mil. Bk. 2-46. Clear, non-flint of the 70s. Listed in my first book which carries a warning on this pattern which all novice collectors should read. I'm showing the celery because the shape is so unusual. Spooner, open sugar $40.00; creamer $85.00; celery $80.00; covered butter $150.00; covered sugar $100.00; handled mug, egg cup $80.00; open compote $65.00; covered compote $100.00. *Boston & Sandwich, opaque white 150% more.*

No. 2049 – BEADED MIRROR – Listed and goblet pictured in my first book. The large plate shown is in the Sandwich Museum. Lately I've seen the goblet in flint also. Flint goblet $45.00; large plate $50.00. *Aka Beaded Medallion, Boston Silver Glass, 1870s.*

No. 1484 – SCALLOPED LINES – Listed and goblet shown in my first book, but here is another large plate from the Sandwich Museum. Plate $40.00. *Sweeney McCluney, 1871.*

WHERE AND WHEN WAS IT MADE?

In another article here I think I've told you why it is absolutely impossible to give an accurate answer to that question. I want to give you a specific case in point. One worker was a man named Davis who worked a time for the Portland Glass Co. and we've found his name entwined in the branches of a Tree of Life compote marker "Portland Glass Co." When Portland Glass Co. folded, he went back to Pittsburgh to another glass company and we find an occasional piece of Shell and Tassel with the Pittsburgh name and Davis on it. We simply do not know within the range of a few years when these patents were used. The life of a patent is long, I believe now it is about that of a copyright which is twenty-nine years and then an extension can be granted for a like period. So you see a patent date does not limit as to time or place.

1533
Beehive

2189
Sherwood

1708
Mid Band

1700
Mid Rib

1703
Applied Bands

2226
Quartered Block

1706
Many Bands
Triple Frosted Band

1753
Small Block
& Prism

No. 1533 – BEE HIVE – Mil. 122. Clear, non-flint of the 80s. Goblet $95.00. *Indiana Tumbler and Goblet (Greentown), 1895.*

No. 2189 – SHERWOOD – Mil. Bk. 2-66. Clear, non-flint of the 80s. Very like TAILORED BAND in my first book, only in that the bowl is slightly more angular and the stem is plain. Goblet $15.00; spooner, open sugar $15.00; creamer $20.00; covered butter $30.00; covered sugar $25.00. These simple geometrics are good to use with any flowered china or in fact, with any which is well decorated with any motif or scene. *Aka Knurled Band.*

No. 1708 – MID BAND – Previously unlisted; clear, non-flint of the early 80s; at least four piece set. Same value as Sherwood above.

No. 1700 – MID RIB – Another previously unlisted, clear flint of the early 80s, same value as Sherwood. It is interesting to see these two designs evolved simply by different use of a line passing through the center.

No. 1706 – TRIPLE FROSTED BAND – Mil. Bk. 2-119. I called this MANY BANDS in my Booklet No. 3, but then I found it in Mil. and I prefer to use existing names. Open sugar, spooner $15.00; goblet (design improves on these erect pieces) $20.00; creamer $25.00; covered butter $35.00; covered sugar $30.00; celery $25.00.

No. 2226 – QUARTERED BLOCK – K. Bk. 2-90. Made in many pieces; priced as Sherwood above; plus flat sauce $6.00; covered compote $50.00; water pitcher $50.00; lamp $90.00; *open compote $45.00. Duncan's #55. There is another pattern using the same name.*

No. 1703 – APPLIED BAND – Hitherto unlisted; clear, non-flint of the 70s. I've never heard of a goblet nor a tumbler. Values same as Sherwood; 4½" flat sauce shown $3.00.

No. 1753 – SMALL BLOCK AND PRISM – Previously unlisted only as I noted it in my Booklet No. 2. A reader wrote in thinking I had confused it with 1752 – THREE STORIES. This is not the case. In the latter the blocks are flatter and the prisms at the base of the bowl are smaller and look as if they were added. In this the prisms seem an integral part of the design. With the two adjacent, the difference is marked. Goblet $25.00; wine $20.00; other values same as Sherwood. Clear, non-flint of the 80s or early 90s.

WHAT SHALL I COLLECT?

I stand at the show, up comes a lady with the prize query, "What shall I collect?" Then it's my turn, "How do you live, how fat is your purse, what are your tastes?" I'd hate to tell you the question I'd really like to ask. If one foolishly takes a half hour trying to show such a one different possibilities, the inevitable answer is, "That isn't what I had in mind."

Patterns fit their surroundings and their owners. We do have a standard rule of design, one plain element, one geometric element, one naturalistic element. But like all standard rules it is best, when broken or at least cracked, by a skillful hand. Plain mat, flowered dishes call for geometric goblet, then there is question of weight, texture and feel of the whole. The formal settings of Chippendale furniture or the like take the simple old flints to advantage; many homes have reproductions of these and the same holds. Many have inherited sets of Haviland which they use, often with this a light weight simple geometric like Diamond Quilted will do the trick as the dishes are flowered.

Recently I saw a gay 90s setting which was very attractive in a pattern of which I think very little, namely Bouquet. It's of the late Victorian era, originally had red paint backing which has been removed. It has large plates, so there were service plates on shocking pink mats. The centerpiece was pink carnations in a Bouquet bowl. I apologized to the pattern; it was effective.

**503
Chandelier**

1661
Straight
Ball and Swirl

1611
Thousand
Eye Band

1614
Elmino

2330
Divided Stem

1721
Inverness

1602
Bow Knot Stem

313
Block Band—
Knob Stem

No. 503 – CHANDELIER – Mil. 163 – L.V. calls it CROWN JEWEL, its original trade name. A clear, non-flint of the early 80s whose pleasing pattern has attracted many collectors and raised its value above that of most patterns of its era. Comes in many pieces, plain and etched, which adds nothing to its value. Flat sauce $15.00; salt dip $20.00; open sugar $25.00; spooner $30.00; tumbler $35.00; celery $45.00; creamer $50.00; pair of salt shakers $70.00; tray for water set $50.00; covered butter $75.00; covered sugar $65.00; covered compotes $95.00; water pitcher $110.00; open compotes $50.00; goblet $85.00. *O'Hara Glass; 1888, U.S. Glass, 1891.*

No. 1661 – STRAIGHT BALL AND SWIRL – Previously unlisted. Not to be confused with the very popular 1616 Ball and Swirl, listed in my first book. In the former, the swirls are curved, here they are straight lines. Same values as remainder of the non-flints of the late 80s and early 90s. Goblet $25.00. *McKee Bros., 1894, reproduced in milk glass.*

No. 1611 – THOUSAND EYE BAND – Mil. Bk. 2-151. Another of this large family of the late 80s in the non-flint; same values. Interesting stem. Wine $10.00.

No. 1614 – ELMINO – Mil. Bk. 2-109. And still another of the clear, non-flints of the late 80s. This one has a most interesting stem; a set of goblets with differing stem interest might be fun to collect. Goblet $20.00; *wine $12.00; with ruby stain $35.00. Ripley & Co., 1880s, U.S. Glass, 1891.*

No. 2330 – DIVIDED STEM – This type of divided stem not previously listed. Clear, non-flint of the 80s but because of this stem structure this goblet brings $40.00.

No. 2332 – TRIPOD – Mil. Bk. 2-17 (not pictured). Has tripod stem but unlike one above, in this, the three legs join directly to the bowl of the goblet, and carry a design; the bowl of the goblet is bulbous and wide. Contemporary of one above. Value $35.00.

No. 1721 – INVERNESS – Mil. Bk. 2-53. Shown in my Booklet No. 5. Non-flint of the early 90s. Comes in all clear with top trimmed in gilt, red and purple. There are thumbprints at the bottom of the goblet bowl. Wine $10.00; goblet $30.00; with gilt 10% more; with purple 10% more; with red 50% more. *A wine has been found in milk glass, making the Thumbprints unseen. OMN: Carolina (preferred).*

No. 1602 – BOW KNOT STEM – Mil. Bk. 2-55. Clear, non-flint of the late 80s or early 90s. Another somewhat interesting stem. Goblet $10.00. *Often found with etching.*

No. 313 – BLOCK BAND-KNOB STEM – Mil. Bk. 2-164. Clear flint of the late 60s. This goblet does not belong on this page nor with these late, non-flint goblets, but unfortunately the number of patterns listed does not exactly fit the number of pages in the book and some have to be tucked out of place. Goblet, clear flint $30.00.

2408
Crowfoot or
Turkey Track

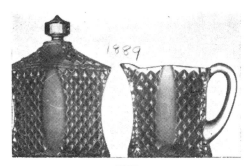

1889
Flat Diamond Box

1818
Tandem Bicycle

2169
Beaded Long Oval

1168
Ribbed Opal

1642
Fagot or Vera

2447
Button Arches—Scalloped
Daisy Red Top

No. 2408 – CROWFOOT OR TURKEY TRACK – L.V.-19 – M. 68 – K. Bk. 3-126 calls it YALE, the original name. This was patented in 1887 for McKee of Pittsburgh, Pa., the page of their catalog shown by Mrs. Kamm is dated 1894, so it shows that patent dates are not too much help in an accurate dating of release of pieces. There were other patterns which producers called Yale so that name is out. Clear, non-flint; flat sauce $12.00; spooner $40.00; open sugar $25.00; open compote $25.00; creamer $40.00; covered butter $80.00; covered compote $75.00; covered sugar $55.00; cake $75.00; goblet $45.00; no wine found. *Crowfoot goblet has been reproduced in clear and amber, also the footed cakestand in clear.*

No. 1889 – FLAT DIAMOND BOX – K. Bk. 3-94. Clear, non-flint of the late 80s. Pattern is square and squat. Covered sugar $35.00; creamer $30.00; covered butter $50.00; bowls $20.00; spooner $30.00. *Fostoria. OMN: Lorraine. Ruby 100% more.*

No. 2169 – BEADED LONG OVAL – Heretofore unlisted. Clear, non-flint of the 80s. So far only butter has been noted but doubtless there is a set. Butter $15.00.

No. 1642 – FAGOT – K. Bk. 4-74 – L.V. 62 calls it VERA. I prefer descriptive names. Clear or clear and frosted of the late 80s, non-flint. Flat sauce $6.00; bowl $15.00; spooner $20.00; open sugar $15.00; open compote $30.00; creamer $30.00; tumbler $20.00; covered butter $35.00; covered sugar $30.00; covered compote $45.00. Prices given are for frosted; all clear 10% less, *ruby 100% more. Robinson Glass, 1893.*

No. 1818 – TANDEM BICYCLE – Mil. 137, shown in my Booklet No. 1. Clear, non-flint of the 80s. All I've ever found was the celery, the wine and the goblet, although there must be more. Wine $25.00; goblet $45.00; celery $45.00. *Made in Nova Scotia.*

No. 1168 – RIBBED OPAL – Listed and shown in my first book. Shown here is the *match holder* which I did not think existed in this pattern; scarcely 2" tall; value $20.00. *Preferred name Beatty Rib. Blue and white opalescent.*

No. 2447 – BUTTON ARCHES – K. Bk. 1-108 – Mil. 1666 calls it SCALLOPED DAISY RED TOP. Clear, and clear with red top, non-flint of the 90s, which comes in many pieces. The demand is for the red top variety for which I quote the prices; goblet $40.00; wine $35.00; creamer $45.00; covered sugar $75.00; mug shown $30.00; souvenir pieces 50% less. *Opaque white and clambroth 50% more.*

2489
Heart Stem

1798
Oval Two Panel

1137
Wheel & Comma

2365
Bissing

2448
Fine Cut Medallion

2363
Melrose

2434
Tiny Fine Cut

1641
Lozenge Band

No. 2489 – HEART STEM – K. Bk. 4-7. As I said in my Booklet No. 2, this piece represents about the worst design I've ever seen in pattern glass; handles are unrelated units, the edge is scalloped, the stem is stippled, the design around the top is of miscellaneous figures, and to top it all, this specimen is etched. If one were looking for a piece to show the decadence of some of the late Victorian art I'd nominate this pattern. To some this sort of thing is quaint or antique or unusual. To me it is confusion. Collectors of heart objects keep its value up to that of other, clear, non-flint of its time, the late 80s or early 90s. Made in sets, including goblets. *Goblet $45.00; cakestand $85.00.*

No. 1798 – OVAL TWO PANEL – Mil. 100 – K. Bk. 5-119 and Bk. 3-113 calls it FLAT OVAL. In Book 3 Kamm shows it with ovals placed horizontally; shown in my Booklet No. 4. I wonder if these are meant to be the same pattern. At any rate, it is an interesting non-flint, clear, glass of the early 80s of the same value as Wheel and Comma. Goblet $35.00.

No. 1137 – WHEEL AND COMMA – K. Bk. 3-5. Clear, non-flint of the 70s. Interesting handles of wheels and commas and finials match handles; shown in my Booklet No. 3. Celery and spooner as well as the sugar have these handles. Unusually lovely etching of roses with plenty of foliage. Goblet $20.00; spooner $18.00; open sugar $15.00; celery $30.00; covered butter $45.00; covered sugar $35.00.

No. 2365 – BISSING – Mil. 172. Clear, non-flint of the late 80s or early 90s. Same values as its contemporaries. *Goblet $10.00; ruby flash $25.00.*

No. 2448 – FINE CUT MEDALLION – K. Bk. 2-43. Clear, non-flint of the late 80s or early 90s. Same values as others of this era. *OMN Grenada, Model Flint Glass. Some glass books have mis-identified Fine Cut Medallion as Greentown's Austrian. They are two different patterns. The "cuts" in Austrian are square shaped. Both the sugar and creamer have oval lids.*

No. 2363 – MELROSE – K. Bk. 3-128 and Bk. 5-47 and pl. 28. Clear, non-flint, made in Ohio and Pennsylvania in the late 80s and early 90s. Same values as others of its time. Covered butter and covered sugar have an interesting collar extending around the top. *Occasionally found in chocolate glass. 6" chocolate compote $225.00. Melrose was manufactured by many firms including Brilliant Glassworks, c 1887; Greensburg Glass Co., c 1889; J.B. Higbee, c 1907; New Martinsville, c 1916; Dugan Glass, c 1915.*

No. 2434 – TINY FINE CUT – Previously unlisted; clear and dark green of the early 90s. Clear wine $15.00; goblet $20.00; decanter $25.00; in dark green 100% additional; *water tray $30.00.*

No. 1642 – LOZENGE BAND – Previously unlisted. Clear, or dark green, non-flint of the early 90s. Wine, goblet $12.00; decanter $25.00; dark green 100% more.

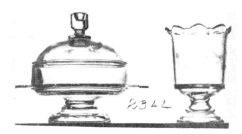

2344
Hill and Dale—Four piece set

1712
Sunken Teardrop

1931
Checkerboard Band

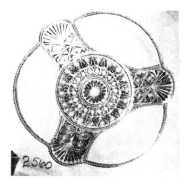

2560
Hartley Plate

No. 2344 – HILL AND DALE – Previously unlisted. Clear, non-flint of the 80s. A time when many of these were made for premiums. Spooner, open sugar $10.00; covered butter $25.00; creamer $20.00; covered sugar $20.00. *Found etched and clear.*

No. 1712 – SUNKEN TEARDROP – K. Bk. 4-26. Shown in my Booklet No. 5. Another four piece set, contemporary of one above; same values.

No. 1931 – CHECKERBOARD BAND – K. Bk. 7-60. This is the spooner from another four piece set, contemporary of the two above; same values as they.

No. 2560 – HARTLEY – Listed in my first book. Plate is sometimes hard to identify; value $25.00. *Hartley found in clear, vaseline, dark amber, blue, and apple green. Vaseline 100% more; blue and apple green 75% more; amber 25% more. Goblet $40.00; wine $35.00; pitcher $65.00; spooner $30.00; celery 40.00. Aka Panelled Diamond Point and Fan; Daisy and Button with Fan. Richards & Hartley, 1887; U.S. Glass, 1891.*

WHO HAS ERRED?
WHO IS THE BETTER STUDENT?

"For he is right, and she is right
And you are right, and I am right
And we are right, and they are right
And all is right as right as right can be."
    –Gilbert and Sullivan in *The Mikado.*

One reads carefully documented statements as to the history of a glass pattern by an author with a yen for meticulous detail and then the history of the same pattern written by an equally careful student and the two do not correspond. One visits our foremost museum, where labelling is done with utmost care and a piece claimed as manufactured in a local factory. You visit an equally fine museum, hundreds of miles distant and find the same piece of glass as manufactured in another far away locale. Then comes a glass magazine with a writer who having found the patent date of the mold thinks the problem is solved and all other attributions are incorrect. Nothing could be further from the truth. When I'm asked where was it made and exactly when and I shy away from an exact answer, it is not that I approve sloppy research. On the contrary, I disapprove faulty, surface scratching research. Patents for molds mean very, very little. There were factories which did nothing but make molds; there were firms that had workmen patent molds, make glass for them, move on to another locale and years later make glass for another firm. Molds were patented in England also at times and this accounts for some English registry marks seen. So you see it is well nigh impossible to accurately assign, date and place of manufacture to a pattern. In the merger of 1892 many of the old patterns were reissued and we do not know whether it is first edition of the 80s or a reissue in the 90s we are getting, so the indefinite one is generally the most accurate one. Patents are readily attainable, my library has a copy of them available for study as do other large cities, but they are only a poor tool at best. So you see, discrimination as to quality is the important factor in the study of glass — not unobtainable detail.

1765
Diamond Medallions

1756
Triple Band & Fan

1646
Pantagraph Band

1482
Tile Band

1614
Prisms & Globules

2426
Pioneer's Victoria

1467
Draped Dia. & Bud
or Looped Ovals

1465
Loop and Chain Band

No. 1765 – DIAMOND MEDALLION – L.V.31 – Mil. 32 – K. Bk. 1-25 calls it FINE CUT AND DIAMOND. In Booklet 3 – Kamm shows it under its original trade name of GRAND *(preferred)*; also shown in my Booklet No. 1. Was on the market in 1885, clear, non-flint, made in many forms and seems quite plentiful. Flat sauce $12.00; goblet $30.00; wine $20.00; spooner $25.00; open sugar $20.00; bowls $20.00; waste bowl $20.00; salt shaker $25.00; footed sauce $12.00; footed covered butter $45.00; celery $30.00; covered sugar $40.00; open compote $25.00; flat covered butter $40.00; 11" plate $30.00; 10" cakestand $45.00; covered compote, water pitcher $55.00.

To above Diamond Medallion pieces added sherbet mug $30.00; decanter, with original stopper $80.00; syrup pitcher $80.00; clear or for red flashing add an extra 150% (rare). *Bryce Higbee, c 1884.*

No. 1756 – TRIPLE BAND AND FAN – Previously unlisted; clear non-flint of 1910. $25.00. *McKee Bros., c 1910.*

No. 1646 – PANTAGRAPH BAND – Mil. Bk. 2-24. Another non-flint, *1880s*, goblet $15.00.

No. 1482 – TILE BAND – Mil. 155. Clear, non-flint of the 80s. I believe this is the pattern to which OWL AND PUSSY CAT CHEESE DISH, shown on dedication pages, belongs. *Goblet $30.00.*

No. 1614 – PRISMS AND GLOBULES – Mil. Bk. 2-140. Clear, non-flint of the 80s. $25.00.

No. 2426 – PIONEER'S VICTORIA – K Bk. 3-83 and K. Bk. 8-64 and pl. 77-78. Goblet clear $25.00; *lemonade pitcher $75.00; ruby 100% more; gold 50% more.*

No. 1467 – LOOPED OVALS – Mil. Bk. 2-147 – L. 164-No. 20. Clear, non-flint of the 80s. $25.00.

No. 1465 – LOOP AND CHAIN BAND – Mil. Bk. 2-122. Clear, non-flint of the 80s. $20.00.

STATES NAMES GIVEN TO PATTERNS

Some dealers and writers have made a fetish of keeping original names or the names of states when they were given to patterns. It can lead to much confusion as some state's names were given to as many as five patterns; the same holds true of original names, different factories gave a different name to the same pattern. A few patterns have retained their name of a state: Washington, New York Honeycomb, Rhode Island, Dakota is Baby Thumbprint, Virginia, (Galloway) besides being the one for which we generally use it was named for three additional states. Hand was named Pennsylvania, Palm and Scroll was Missouri. Beaded Loop was Missouri, Skilton is Oregon, Jewel with Dew Drop is Kansas, Delaware and Four Petal Flower are the same. I'm sure we can find more practical ways to honor our states than to cause confusion among collectors.

Goblet

Compote

1621
York Herringbone

1627
Crescent Band

1883
Quihote

1620
Frazier

1649
Lace Band

1715
Facetted Rosette Band

1717
Corrigan

No. 1621 – YORK HERRINGBONE – Mil. 45. Clear, non-flint of the late 80s. As the picture of the goblet and small covered compote show, this pattern is pleasing in design even though it is quite late; this fact raises it about 20% above the ordinary ones of the era. Goblet, clear $35.00; *covered compote $75.00; tumbler $30.00; pitcher $75.00. Aka Scalloped Swirl, U.S. Glass (Ripley), 1892. Ruby 100% more.*

No. 1627 – CRESCENT BAND – Another, non-flint of the same era and very much like York Herringbone with which it would combine nicely; of same value as the former. This piece was sent to me by an intelligent student of glass, Mr. Jack Kroehne of La Crueces, New Mexico. *Circa 1880 – 90.*

No. 1883 – QUIHOTE – Mil. Bk. 2-89. Another of the non-flints of same era and same quality and same value as the two above. It comes flashed with red and I suspect the other two are the same. *Tarentum, OMN: Columbia, c 1889. Goblet $35.00; ruby $90.00.*

No. 1620 – FRAZIER – Another of the non-flints of the early 90s, this one is slightly stiffer and not as graceful in the design so falls in the ordinary class as to values. Red flashing 100% additional. *U.S. Glass #15087. Aka Diamond Mat Band.* Goblet $15.00; ruby $30.00.

No. 1649 – LACE BAND – M. Bk. 2-3. Clear, non-flint of the 80s. Goblet, wine $8.00; spooner, open sugar $8.00; covered butter $15.00; covered sugar $15.00. *Imperial Glass Co., c 1902 – 10. Aka Optic Flute. Clear $15.00; ruby $35.00.*

No. 1715 – FACETTED ROSETTE BAND – Mil. Bk. 2-3 – K. Bk. 6-65 calls it BOX IN BOX (preferred). Shown in my Booklet No. 5. Clear, non-flint of the 80s. *Riverside #420. Clear $95.00; ruby $135.00.*

No. 1717 – CORRIGAN – Mil. Bk. 2-39. Shown in my Booklet No. 5; clear, non-flint of the 80s. As interesting as the flyer for whom it was named. Stem would make it fitting for collection of unusual stemmed goblets; goblet $40.00; wine $25.00; cake stand, $125.00. The last four goblets on this page would go together nicely. *Dalzell, Gilmore & Leighton Glass Co., c 1890.*

2374
Duncan Block

1683
Nail

1760
Millard

2162
Diamond Band with
Panels

1882
Truncated Cube

2207
Britannic

1881
Block & Spear Point

1690
Electric

No. 2374 – DUNCAN BLOCK – Mil. Bk. 2-78 calls it YOKED SPEAR POINT – K. Bk. 3-130 calls it SWAG BLOCK – L.V. 71 calls it DUNCAN BLOCK, as it was made in one of the Duncan factories in Pennsylvania in the early 90s. Non-flint, all clear, or clear with red flashing. Footed sauce $10.00; goblet $35.00; open sugar $20.00; tumbler $25.00; bowl $20.00; celery $40.00; open compote $25.00; butter $50.00; covered sugar $45.00; covered compote $50.00; water pitcher $75.00; with amber or red flashing an additional 100%. *OMN: #326. Aka Block, Swag Block, Waffle Variant. U.S. Glass, 1891.*

No. 1683 – NAIL – Listed and compote pictured in my first book, but I felt a better picture was needed. Goblet, clear $45.00; ruby $95.00. *Ripley, 1880s. U.S. Glass #15002, c 1891.*

No. 1760 – MILLARD – L.V.-42 and on plate 52 shows the same thing flashed with color and calls it MILLARD VARIATION. Mil. Bk. 2-55 shows it with the red panels and calls it SOUVENIR WITH RED PANELS. It was a nice gesture for Mrs. Lee to name a pattern for Dr. Millard just as it was equally thoughtful of the good doctor to name that lovely flint pattern for Ruth Webb Lee; collectors and dealers owe them both a debt of gratitude and though they have both been gone for years, their work is ever fresh in our memory. So it is another of the late ones, pleasing design, made in many forms. Clear: flat sauce $5.00; footed sauce, relish trays, custard cups $7.00; goblet $35.00; spooner $25.00; open sugar $12.00; pair salt and pepper shakers $40.00; creamer $20.00; tumbler $15.00; cruet $45.00; covered butter $50.00; covered sugar $45.00; large plate $20.00; covered compote $50.00; water pitcher $80.00; cakestands, small $45.00; large $55.00; with amber flashing 50% additional; with red flashing 100% additional Etched or not does not alter value. *U.S. Glass #15016, c 1893.*

No. 2162 – DIAMOND BAND WITH PANELS – Heretofore unlisted. Clear and red flashed of the early 90s, non-flint. Because this pattern is not known, value would be 10% less than Millard, above. This goblet is from the collection of the Willard Mellvilles of Wisconsin. *Co-operative Flint Glass Co. OMN: Radiant, c 1908. Goblet $30.00; ruby $75.00.*

No. 1882 – TRUNCATED CUBE – Mil. Bk. 2-35. Clear and clear and red flashed, non-flint of the early 90s; values same as the pattern, Millard. *Thompson Glass #77, c 1894. Goblet $25.00; ruby $40.00; amber $55.00 (scarce).*

No. 2207 – BRITTANIC – K. Bk. 4-71. Clear and clear flashed with red, made in 1895; same values as pattern, Millard.

No. 1881 – BLOCK AND SPEAR POINT – Mil. 96. Clear, non-flint of the 80s. Wine $10.00; goblet $15.00.

No. 1690 – ELECTRIC – K. Bk. 3-78. Clear, non-flint of the late 80s or early 90s; goblet $15.00; complete set of many pieces. *Scarce. U.S. Glass #15038, c 1896. Goblet $85.00; ruby $125.00.*

2529
Crocesus Cov. Sugar and Creamer

2212
Whitton

2520
Royal Crystal

1851
Double Red Block

1848
Red Block and Lattice

2518
Srcoll and Cane Band

2471
Crossed Ovals

No. 2529 – CROESUS – Listed in my first book; shown in my Booklet No. 5. *Riverside Glass. Butter reproduced. Currently in great demand. Covered sugar $100.00, green $150.00, amethyst $200.00, creamer $60.00, green $75.00, amethyst $165.00.*

No. 2212 – WHITTON – Clear and clear flashed with red of the early 90s. There are some to whom any piece with a dash of color is highly desirable and as a result some of these very late patterns are bringing more than they are worth. They can, however, be used most effectively; the red flashed one is very pleasing with flow blue china, and the amber can be most effective with sepia Staffordshire. This pattern is fairly good design, and Ruby Thumbprint is simple and excellent, but I'm sorry to report, is the object of speculation at present. Values: goblet $30.00; wine $20.00; creamer $20.00; covered butter $35.00; spooner $20.00; open sugar $12.00; covered sugar $35.00; flashed with red an additional 100%. *Aka Heavy Gothic. Columbia Glass c, 1890; U.S. Glass #15014, c 1891.*

No. 2520 – ROYAL CRYSTAL – M. 165 – L.V. 57. Another of the non-flints of the early 90s which comes in all clear and clear flashed with red and I believe, amber. Flat sauce $10.00; spooner $30.00; open sugar $20.00; creamer $35.00; celery $40.00; covered butter $75.00; covered sugar $75.00; goblet $50.00. *Tarentum's Atlanta, c 1894. Ruby stain 100% more.*

No. 1852 – DOUBLE RED BLOCK – Mil. Bk. 2-93. In Book 1-136 Millard lists same goblet in clear calling it HEXAGON BLOCK. Clear and clear flashed in color of the early 90s; same values as Royal Crystal..

No. 1848 – RED BLOCK AND LATTICE – Mil. Bk. 3-92. Clear non-flint, heavy glass of the early 90s, clear and clear flashed with color of the early 90s. At first glance one might think this to be the same as Red Block with another row added, but on looking closer she sees there is another unit of triangles there. Same values as other members of family, above. *Pioneer Glass Co., c 1890s. Aka Pioneer #9, Button & Star. Goblet $45.00; ruby $95.00.*

No. 2518 – SCROLL WITH CANE BAND – K. Bk. 92. Clear, non-flint, heavy glass of the early 90s, comes flashed with red and amber and I'd not be surprised to find any of these flashed in a rare dark blue. I don't believe there is a goblet, but there is a tumbler, open sugar shown, there is also an individual creamer. Clear: spooner $35.00; open sugar $25.00; creamer $35.00; individual creamer $20.00; covered butter $70.00; tumbler $20.00; covered sugar $45.00; flashed with red or amber 100% additional; *toothpick $35.00. West Virginia Glass, 1894.*

No. 2471 – CROSSED OVALS – Clear, non-flint of the early 1880s. Wine (shown) goblet $15.00.

2234
Illusion

1835
Cat's Eye

1657
Stippled Diamond Band

2214
Triangles and Fans

2392
Circle and Dot

1629
Dickery Dock

2504
Manhattan

2380
Bull's Eye and
Diamond Quilted

No. 2234 – ILLUSION – Mil. Bk. 2-59. Clear, non-flint of the 80s; $25.00.

No. 1835 – CAT'S EYE – Mil. Bk. 2-141. Clear and goblet shown is amber, non-flint of the 80s. Same values with additional added percent of color. The fact that the one has been seen in colors, shows that probably most of the goblet colors were made. $20.00. *Clear, colors usual percentage more!*

No. 1657 – STIPPLED DIAMOND BAND – Mil. Bk. 2-17–L page 164–No. 8. Another of the 80s. Same values. *Goblet $20.00.*

No. 2214 – TRIANGLES AND FANS – Mil. Bk. 2-119. Another of the non-flints; same era, same values. *Circa 1885.*

No. 2392 – CIRCLE AND DOT – Listed but not pictured in my first book. *1880s, goblet $25.00.*

No. 1629 – DICKERY DOCK – Mil. Bk. 2-11. Clear, non-flint of the 70s. *Goblet $15.00.*

No. 2504 – MANHATTAN – K. Bk. 2-11. Clear and ruby, same values as Millard. *Reproduced in 1950s. U.S. glass, 1901, #15078. Goblet $25.00; maiden's blush $75.00; ruby stain $75.00. Green is a reproduction, as is amber.*

No. 2380 – BULL'S EYE AND DIAMOND QUILTED – Mil. Bk. 2-118. Clear, non-flint of the mid 80s; goblet $20.00.

1738
Double Fan

1768
Mikado Fan

1759
Diamond Mirror

1860
Fancy Diamonds

2422
Diamonds in Diamonds

2513
Panelled Thumbprint

2235
Group Thumbprint

1868
Divided Squares

No. 1738 – DOUBLE FAN – K. Bk. 1-40. Clear, non-flint of the 90s. Spooner, open sugar $12.00; celery (shown), creamer $25.00; covered butter $25.00; covered sugar $25.00; *ruby stain 50% more.*

No. 1733 – TRIMMED DOUBLE FAN – (Not pictured). L.V. 57 calls it the same as the pattern above, but in this the fans are outlined by bands filled with a zig-zag design, and the erect pieces are footed, not flat, as in the case of the one above. Clear, non-flint of the late 80s or early 90s and values are the same as those of its contemporaries. Made in Pennsylvania.

No. 1768 – MIKADO FAN – Mil. 128. Clear, non-flint of late 80s; $35.00.

No. 1759 – DIAMOND MIRROR – Mil. Bk. 2-53. And still another of the non-flints of the same era, $125.00. *Fostoria, c 1889.*

No. 1860 – FANCY DIAMONDS – Previously unlisted, another of this large family; $15.00. *Aka Diagonal Bead Bands, Model Flint Glass Co., c 1890.*

No. 2422 – DIAMONDS IN DIAMOND – Mil. 167. L.V. 30 calls it DIAMONDS. Another of the same era. *Goblet $20.00; ruffled compote $25.00.*

No. 2513 – PANELLED THUMBPRINT – K. Bk. 1-111. Clear, non-flint of the early 80s, same values.

No. 2235 – GROUP THUMBPRINT – Not previously listed, non-flint early 80s, same values.

No. 2238 – COLUMNED THUMBPRINT – K. Bk. 5-71 (Not pictured). Clear, non-flint of the early 90s, very like one listed above only this has one single line separating thumbprints from diamond units, which are made of very fine diamonds. Same values.

No. 1868 – DIVIDED SQUARES – Previously unlisted. I've seen this in tumblers and the goblet shown, which belongs to the Willard Melvilles of Wisconsin; both were frosted with an amber rim, although I have no doubt that it was made in all clear also. It is a non-flint of the 80s and in the clear it would be of the same value as the others of this time, in the frosted and amber combination an added 100%. *Goblet $45.00. Aka Hobbs Block. Hobbs, Brockunier & Co. #330, c 1889. Amber rim with frosted body $155.00; amber rim with clear body $140.00.*

1981
Tandem Diamonds
& Thumprints

2231
Pitcairn

1990
Panelled Herringbone

1988
Quill Band

1639
Spear Point and
Daisy Band

2210
Galaxy

1936
Loop & Pyramids

1976
Churchill

No. 1981 – TANDEM DIAMOND AND THUMBPRINT – Mil. Bk. 2-4. Clear non-flint of the early 80s. Values the same as all of the others of this time. Shown in my Booklet No. 1. *Burlington Glass Works, c 1880. Creamer $30.00.*

No. 2231 – PITCAIRN – Mil. Bk. 2-52. Another one of these non-flints of the early 80s, comes all clear and clear and frosted, values for all clear same as the others of its time, for frosted add another 10%. *King Glass Co. #31, c 1880. Goblet, clear $35.00.*

No. 1990 – PANELLED HERRINGBONE – is what most dealers call this and that is the name K. Bk. 4-114 gives to a creamer which does not look too much like the Panelled Herringbone creamer in shape but line drawings can be inaccurate. Mil. Bk. 2-137 calls it PRISM AND HERRINGBONE. Clear and dark green of the 90s; value for clear same as other clear of era but for the dark green add at least another 100%. Sauce dishes, bowls and plates are square in outline. *Circa 1890s. Goblet $30.00, ruby stain $65.00, green %50.00.*

No. 1988 – QUILL BAND – Another non-flint very like one above, only this does not have the tiny beads lining the panels. Clear, values same as the other clear ones.

No. 1639 – SPEAR POINT AND DAISY BAND – Mil. Bk. 2-07. A more interesting member of this late non-flint family, better design will increase its value about 10%. *Specialty Glass Co., c 1880s, pattern "E." Goblet $12.00.*

No. 2210 – GALAXY – Another design of same era which carries a little more design interest. Shown in my Booklet No. 5. Mil. Bk. 2-67. $25.00.

No. 1936 – LOOP AND PYRAMIDS – Mil. Bk. 2-79. The goblet is quite good design for so late, but the creamer, sugar, etc., are wretched. Goblet $15.00; other pieces same values. *Tarentum Glass Co. #292, c 1901.*

No. 1976 – CHURCHILL – M. 102. A block type goblet of the early 80s and lacking all the distinction of the person whose name it bears. Clear, non-flint, valued as the others of this era. *Goblet $25.00.*

513
Prism Banded Top

2261
Fine Pleat

1579
Overall Lattice—
Moesser

2264
Panelled Ladder

1841
Staggered Prism

2263
Trellis

2273
Opposing Drops

2512
Reardon

No. 513 – PRISM-BANDED TOP – Mil. Bk. 2-145. No relative of the early flint Prism, this is a clear, non-flint of the mid or late 80s. Probably made in set of many pieces as most of these late geometric patterns were and their values are all about the same; flat sauce $6.00; footed sauce $8.00; bowls $10.00; spooner $15.00; open sugar $10.00; creamer $20.00; open compote $20.00; covered butter $35.00; covered sugar $30.00; covered compotes $40.00.

No. 2261 – FINE PLEAT – Mil. Bk. 2-135. Another clear, non-flint of the 80s. Values same as Banded Top Prism, above. Goblet $15.00.

No. 1579 – OVERALL LATTICE – K. Bk. 2-43 – Mil. Bk. 2-107 calls it MOESSER. Clear, non-flint. *1897. Indiana Tumbler & Goblet (Greentown) #38. Goblet $65.00; pitcher $120.00; ruby add 50%.*

No. 2264 – PANELLED LADDER – Mil. Bk. 2-3. Another of the same time, same kind. *Goblet $15.00.*

No. 1841 – STAGGERED PRISM – Mil. 55. Clear, non-flint, same as the others. *Goblet $25.00.*

No. 2263 – TRELLIS – Mil. 91 – K. Bk. 8-24 calls it LATTICE AND LENS. Still another of the same, non-flint geometrics, same values as Banded Top Prism.

No. 2273 – OPPOSING DROPS – Heretofore unlisted; another of the same group; same values.

No. 2512 – REARDON – Mil. 172. Another of the non-flint; same values. Very similar to Chain Thumbprints in my first book, only in that there are more lines between the chains of the prints which, too, vary slightly in shape from these. Same value as the others of these families. *Found with etching.*

PRICES OF GLASS

I have received many inquiries regarding the price of a piece in a pattern which is listed but the price of that piece is not. For instance a writer asks the price of a bowl in a pattern in which I've listed prices of other pieces but not of bowl. Instead of writing me I suggest she take time and find a similarly priced pattern which has a bowl listed. Remember my prices are not meant to be strictly limited dollar and cents value, they are guide lines and are supposed to be used as such.

How do you arrive at prices? I'm frequently asked. Prices are based primarily on demand for an article. When one finds a wanted article in short supply, she knows that short supply can command a price. Frequently we find a rare article in which very few are interested, such a piece will not command money.

The value of pieces of glass change from time to time as usage for certain pieces gain in popularity. Following is a list of some popular present usages which are causing scarcity and raising prices of articles listed:

Tumblers — the smartest new fashioned way to serve an "old fashioned."
Covered compotes — used on counter wash stands in bathrooms and on dining room tables and buffets as permanent centerpieces.
Water pitcher — their decorative possibilities have been recognized and they are being used as vases. Even empty a beautiful pitcher is decorative.
Covered sugars, now called candy jars — shows what they are used for.
Open sugars, plain band at top, called Buttermilk — used as schooners, for iced tea, etc.; immensely popular and practical.
Cakestands — frequently inverted and used as a centerpiece.
Wines, fast disappearing, needed for service, cordials are about gone.

1939
Side Wheeler

2441
Stippled Loop

1907
Panelled Hexagons

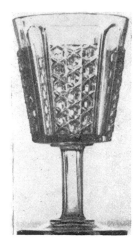

1975
Prisms & Hexagons

1384
Petalled Medallion

2393
Gathered Knot

1480
Pleat Band and
Diamond

2172
Beatrice

No. 1939 – SIDE WHEELER – K. Bk. 5-31. Clear, non-flint of the 80s. *Goblet $30.00.*

No. 2441 – STIPPLED LOOP – Mil. Bk. 2-27. Clear, non-flint of the early 80s; listed but not pictured in my first book. *Goblet $20.00.*

No. 1907 – PANELLED HEXAGONS – Mil. Bk. 2-5 calls this PANELLED ARGUS but because it is a clear non-flint of the late 80s, in no way related to the early Argus flint family I've called it by a better descriptive name, for there are no indentations, and no thumbprints, but raised hexagons in these vertical rows. Shown in my Booklet No. 1. *McKee Bros., c 1886. Clear goblet $20.00, apple green $45.00, blue $45.00.*

No. 1975 – PRISMS AND HEXAGONS – Unlisted until shown in my Booklet No. 3. Contemporary of these other non-flints of the 80s, same values.

No. 1384 – PETALLED MEDALLION – Previously unlisted, non-flint of the 80s. *OMN: Brilliant. Riverside Glass, c 1895. 100% more for amber or ruby stain; goblet $35.00.*

No. 2393 – GATHERED KNOT – Mil. Bk. 2-104. Clear, non-flint of the 90s, made in many pieces; K. Bk. 7-39 shows it, calling it IMPERIAL No. 3. In addition to above pieces valued this has salt shakers, pair $30.00; sugar shaker $40.00; covered jam jar $75.00; syrup jug $100.00. This pattern was still in production into the early 1900s as many of these late ones were. *Goblet $25.00. Imperial Glass Co., #03, c 1903.*

No. 1480 – PLEAT BAND AND DIAMOND – Previously unlisted, another of these late, non-flints. *Goblet $20.00.*

No. 2173 – BEATRICE – Mil. 158. Another of the same family of non-flints. *Goblet $15.00.*

2564
Jeter D. & B.

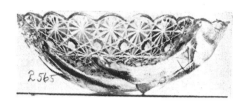

2565
D & B—Mitted Hand Bowl

2561
Belmont Creamer

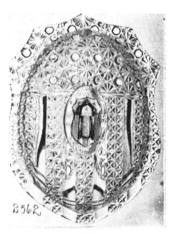

2562
Banner Butter Dish

2565

2147
Beaded Loop

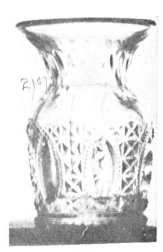

2147
Beaded Loop Toothpick

2184
Clio Plate

No. 2564 – JETER DAISY AND BUTTON – Mil. 129. One of the rare, clear, non-flint forms of the well known family and happily one, which has not been reproduced. All I've seen is the goblet $75.00.

No. 2565 – MITTED HAND BOWL – (two views shown). An Indiana glass product; deep bowl, about 6" in length, with gloved hand holding base. Also a Daisy and Button novelty product in demand which has not been reproduced to date and which I've seen only in clear. Most reproductions come out in color as the makers figure that is what the public craves; a certain element of that public does just that and frequently pays too dearly in satisfying its longing. Non-flint of the late 80s, value $60.00. *Indiana Tumbler & Goblet (Greentown). Nile green or chocolate $600.00+.*

No. 2561 – BELMONT – K. Bk. 6-56 and pl. 17. Made in 1886 at Bellaire, Ohio, at the Belmont Glass Works. Finials are a sphere through which a bar passes, and this whole is surmounted by a tiny knob. Really a very fussy form of Daisy and Button in the clear and another of which there has been no reproduction to date. Non-flint, of course, creamer $45.00; covered butter $100.00; covered sugar $50.00. *Canary 100% more, amber 50% more.*

No. 2562 – BANNER BUTTER DISH – L.V. 76. Clear, non-flint Daisy and Button, novelty butter dish of the 80s and another which I've never seen reproduced. What a nice candy dish for the coffee table in the American home. Dish $200.00.

No. 2147 – BEADED LOOP – L. 76 – M. 82 – K. Bk. 3-8 and in Bk. 8-18 shows it as it was reissued in 1907 under the trade name of OREGON *(preferred name)*. It was made in two forms, the flat, awkward type and a footed, more graceful one. It was first made in the 80s, by whom I know not, but evidently by one of the smaller firms which the U.S. Glass Co. took over. Flat sauce $10.00; bowls $20.00 – 45.00; toothpicks $65.00; relish $20.00; footed sauce $15.00; handled mug $55.00; vase toothpick (shown) $65.00; footed spooner $45.00; footed open sugar $15.00; tumbler $45.00; goblet $45.00; flat covered sugar $45.00; celery, creamer $40.00; 6" cakestand $65.00; open compotes $75.00; syrup pitcher $125.00; cruet, 8" $85.00; cakestand, $100.00; footed covered sugar $85.00; water pitcher, $125.00; large covered compotes $95.00 – 120.00. *U.S. Glass States pattern #15074, c 1901. With ruby or green stain add 300%.*

No. 2184 – CLIO – L.V. 46. Non-flint, made by Challinor Taylor of Tarentum, Pennsylvania, in the late 70s or early 80s, in clear and colors. Has not been reproduced. Flat sauce $10.00; collared base sauce, $12.00; bowls $15.00; spooner, $25.00; open sugar, $25.00; collared base bowls $20.00; creamer $35.00; 7" plate $18.00; open compote $25.00; covered butter $45.00; celery $35.00; 10" plate $25.00; covered sugar $35.00; tall covered compote $75.00. Should be a tumbler. *Aka Hanover. Richards & Hartley Glass Co. 1888; U.S. Glass, 1891. Amber add 25%; blue add 50%; canary add 100%.*

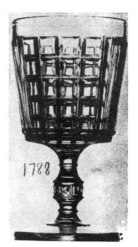

1854
Prism with
Double Block Band

1898
Chadwick

1788
Two Panel Waffle—Two Views

1892
Fibber Block

1893
Pulaski Cube

1895
Pointed Cube

446
Mitered Thumbprint

No. 1854 – PRISM WITH DOUBLE BLOCK BAND – Mil. Bk. 2-84. Clear, non-flint of the 80s; $20.00.

No. 1898 – CHADWICK – Mil. Bk. 2-73. Clear, non-flint of the 80s; same values. $20.00.

No. 1892 – FIBBER BLOCK – Mil. 90. Another clear, non-flint of the 80s; same values. $20.00.

No. 1788 – TWO PANEL WAFFLE – Mil. 105. Clear, non-flint of the 80s; same value; no relation to the early flint Waffle family. Two views shown. $25.00.

No. 1893 – PULASKI CUBE – Mil. 90. Another one of the non-flints in clear of the 80s. $25.00.

No. 1895 – POINTED CUBE – Previously unlisted. Clear and frosted, non-flint of the 80s; wine shown; value same only 10% additional for frosting. $25.00. *English?*

No. 446 – MITERED THUMBPRINT – Mil. 56 and on plate 163, Millard shows the same thing again and calls it MIOTIN WITH ALMOND THUMBPRINTS. Clear, non-flint of the 80s, same values. $25.00.

MIDNIGHT MEDITATION

It had been a busy day and a fruitful one; I was up at the crack of dawn and with my helper drove about one hundred fifty miles to be at a show when it opened and find treasures. I worked carefully, albeit swiftly, and made many purchases, passed up several others as commonplace, defective or fake. I was just about finished when I met a collector who said, "What chance has the ordinary collector got with you on the floor buying?" "I'm buying for just that same ordinary collector," I told him, "that's what he wants me to do."

As I walked through the aisles of that show I spotted numerous pitfalls for unwary buyers. I saw a beautiful square Shell and Tassel covered sugar, but the finial had a large chip of which the dealer was not aware. In another booth I saw a strangely shaped Wildflower dish, covered; upon investigation I found a chipped celery had been ground and a sugar bowl cover fitted to it; in the booth of a specialist in another line I saw fake colored Hobnail; another dealer called me to see her unusual Lion jam jar which had a cover, made of old Mason jar opener type contraption, which an ingenious man had made. All of these changes had ruined the value of the original article. They were being offered as rarities. At another booth was a Bellflower goblet like one I had just returned to a picker as not clear but stained. There was much glass not old enough to be reproduced, no Early American Pattern Glass by any stretch of the imagination. As I sat musing the day's work, I could not help but feel that the antique world is full of pitfalls for the novice and he should be willing to pay the experienced dealer for time spent in guidance and avoidance of these. But please keep your eyes open; and read, read, read, read! Reading is better than asking questions; you will always be told it is old; you will probably be told it is rare if you note it is strange; many are honest but have themselves been fooled, so read, read, read! That's the conclusion I come to in my past midnight meditation.

1979
Panelled
Diamond Cross

1910
Cadmus

2258
Panelled Lattice

228
Panelled
Flattened Sawtooth

1982
Barred Daisy

1658
Thayer

1937
Prism and
Broken Column

2192
Quilted Fan Top

No. 1979 – PANELLED DIAMOND CROSS – Mil. Bk. 2-162 – K. Bk. 2-24 calls it HEAVY PANELLED FINE CUT. I believe this pattern to go to the mid 80s because it carries the footed creamers and more attention is given to design and manufacture. May be found with the bars in color. Goblet, wine $20.00; creamer $20.00; spooner $18.00; open sugar $10.00; covered butter $25.00; covered sugar $25.00. *George Duncan & Sons, 1883; U.S. Glass, 1891. Amber, canary 100% more.*

No. 1910 – CADMUS – Clear, non-flint of *1902. Beaumont Glass Co., c 1902. Goblet $25.00, color $55.00.*

No. 2258 – PANELLED LATTICE – Mil. Bk. 2-85. Clear, 1870s. Goblet $45.00.

No. 228 – PANELLED FLATTENED SAWTOOTH – Mil Bk. 2-143. NOTE. This goblet does not belong here but in the front pages with the early flints, but I put it here because it illustrates a point so well. Compare it with Panelled Lattice; note the vertical separation lines are made by four lines of two decorative types in the Lattice; in the early flint, one strong, simple, vertical line tells the story. In the later goblet with its imitation "cut glass" look, the diamonds are a confused jumble; in the early goblet, they are one bold, large unit. Goblet $55.00.

No. 1982 – BARRED DAISY – Mil. 27. Clear, non-flint of the mid 80s; goblet $20.00. *Probably a jelly container.*

No. 1658 – THAYER – Mil. 144. Clear, non-flint of the mid 80s; goblet $25.00.

No. 1937 – PRISM AND BROKEN COLUMN – Mil. 106. Clear, non-flint of the mid 80s; goblet $20.00.

No. 2192 – QUILTED FAN TOP – Mil. Bk. 2-56 – K. Bk. 3-79 calls it SHEPHERD'S PLAID. Clear, non-flint of the early 90s, made in sets. Goblet $25.00; wine $20.00; spooner $20.00; open sugar $10.00; creamer $25.00; covered butter $45.00; covered sugar $35.00.

A QUESTIONABLE SOURCE OF INFORMATION

It is true that one cannot pay too much heed to all that she reads, especially if she does not choose her reading with discrimination and watch date of latest copyright or printing, but there is a much worse, deeper, more sinister danger. This is the "grapevine" or Sairey Gamp type of information, the "hot tip" of the innermost circle of the "in-the-know" group. Because some think carnival glass will some day have a big future and have gone about gathering all they could find, the price has risen beyond all semblance to real value. Now for another item. The grapevine has the word — it's cobalt blue glass. Very scientific, you know. The cobalt is used in bombs for treating cancer and you know what that means? The sad truth will come from your chemist friend; all that is related in the two products is the six letters used in spelling the word. So I fear your Shirley Temple mugs, creamers and other late dark blue ware may not bring you fame and fortune after all. Is there any one more gullible than a bargain hunter?

2216
Loops and Drops

1745
Netted Arches
and Prisms

1765
Orinocho

2272
Herringbone Rib

2269
Cryptic
Zippered Block

2270
Open Cryptic

1742
Double Diamond
Panels

1744
Ovals and Fine Pleat

No. 2216 – LOOPS AND DROPS – Clear, non-flint of the 90s. *New Jersey (preferred). U.S. Glass Co., c 1900 #15070.* Goblet $45.00, *gold trim $75.00, ruby stain $225.00.*

No. 1745 – NETTED ARCHES AND PRISMS – Heretofore unlisted member of this large family of clear, non-flint glass of the 80s; $20.00.

No. 1765 – ORINOCHO – Mil. Bk. 2-119. More pieces of this have been seen. Flat sauce $6.00; creamer $20.00; goblet $20.00; quality of glass not too good.

No. 2272 – HERRINGBONE RIB – Mil. Bk. 2-118. Clear, non-flint of the late 70s. An interesting pattern with these ribs extending out from the surface of the glass. Goblet $200.00; emerald green $285.00, *cakestand $250.00, cup $95.00. Indiana Tumbler & Goblet (Greentown). Rare in emerald green, amber.*

No. 2269 – ZIPPERED BLOCK – K. BK. 3-131 – Mil. Bk. 2-123 calls it CRYPTIC. Clear, non-flint of the late 90s; $35.00 clear; ruby $75.00.

No. 2270 – OPEN CRYPTIC – Not listed until shown in my Booklet No. 5. Clear, non-flint of the late 90s. Same values as Cryptic, above.

No. 1742 – DOUBLE DIAMOND PANELS – Mil. Bk. 2-4. It is interesting to see the different variations of the diamonds motif that were used. Same value as for other clear, non-flints of the 80s. *Goblet $25.00.*

No. 1744 – OVALS AND FINE PLEAT – Mil. Bk. 2-144. Clear, non-flint of the 80s; design here is more interesting again. *Goblet $20.00.*

WHAT'S WRONG WITH "CUT GLASS" CARNIVAL GLASS?

Nothing, if it is the only thing which satisfies you and you are not buying it as a fad or to make money. First, let me explain that by "cut glass" I do not mean the early glass which was trimmed with a restrained type of cutting, but the heavy all-over cut ware so prevalent in th late 90s and early 1900s. This was the end of the Victorian era, a time marked by much that was in poor taste and much that was over decorated. At times I'm taken to task for my attitude to select the good, forget the other. Just recently I was cornered at a show by a dealer who argued, "Who are you to set standard? Think of the number of people who enjoy these things; think of the amount of money that changes hands for them each year."

Yes, I freely admit I'm not capable of setting standards and I do not pretend to do it. Just check the shops and the advertisements and the high class shows and see how much of this type of ware you see. I don't believe a pianist like Van Clibern, for instance, set the standard for the type of music he plays; hundreds do not enjoy this type, they want rock and roll. Think of the fortunes that have been made and spent for popular music that lived but a few years; the great masters live forever. No, popular taste and money made is not the answer to lasting worth. No one museum sets standards; they are an accumulation of generations of study and learning.

Our dealer went on, "You condemn carnival glass as gaudy, yet there are the colors of the sunset." Yes, there are those colors on a canvas as big as the world, softened by a universe of atmosphere. If one has fewer nerve endings, he may need harsh color, or more than ordinary sparkle to get any sensation, and he may need this as the same type of person is apt to be missing a sense of line and proportion and design which these things so often lack; for him it is all right. An occasional piece, such as the rather clever Orange Tree, might be used for color, or an occasional piece of "cut glass" for sparkle, might be used but when the real reason for collecting or selling these wares is the profit or popularity motif, it's all wrong.

2260
Serrated Rib and Finecut

2535
Panelled English
Hob with Prisms

2538
Imperial

2483
Panelled Diamonds
and Fine Cut—Carmen

2211
Dotted Loop

2425
Amboy

2420
Cane Medallion

1771
Spalding

NO. 2260 – SERRATED RIB AND FINE CUT – Mil. Bk. 2-153. Clear, non-flint of the late 80s or early 90s; goblet $15.00. *Comes in straight sided or barrel shaped.*

No. 2535 – PANELLED ENGLISH HOBNAIL WITH PRISMS – Mil. 111. Clear, non-flint of the early 90s; attractive and highly collectible available in many forms; also known as Duncan and Miller, #42; goblet $40.00; tumbler $25.00; wine $30.00; cordial $32.00; champagne $35.00; water pitcher $65.00; covered butter $75.00; and sugar $50.00; spooner $25.00; creamer $30.00; also found in gold gilt trim and ruby, add 50%. *Mardi Gras preferred name.*

No. 2538 – IMPERIAL – No. 261 – K. Bk. 7-10. Clear, non-flint of the 1900s made by Imperial Glass Co. of Ohio, in many pieces. Pieces are more pleasing in outline than most glass of this late date. Wine, goblet, tumbler $20.00; flat sauce $8.00; footed sauce $10.00; relish $12.00; bowls, celery tray $12.00; spooner $18.00; open sugar $15.00; covered butter $30.00; creamer $25.00; scalloped edge open compote $20.00; covered sugar $25.00. *Imperial #261.*

No. 2483 – PANELLED DIAMOND AND FINE-CUT – Mil. Bk. 2-116 – CARMEN – L.V. 37 and K. Bk. 5-121. Brilliant, clear and clear flashed with yellow, made by Fostoria in West Virginia, in *1901* in many pieces. Sauce dishes $6.00; celery tray $12.00; berry bowls $10.00; rectangular dishes $10.00; spooner $15.00; open sugar $12.00; creamer (same shape as tankard water pitcher) $20.00; covered butter, water pitcher, covered sugar $20.00. Yellow flashing 15% additional. Better in quality and line than most glass of this era.

No. 2211 – DOTTED LOOP – K. Bk. 6-16. Clear, non-flint of the early 90s; wine $20.00; goblet $25.00; *plate $18.00.*

No. 2425 – AMBOY – Mil. Bk. 2-27. Clear, non-flint of the late 80s; goblet $15.00.

No. 2420 – CANE MEDALLION – K. Bk. 1-91. Clear, non-flint of the early 90s; creamer is covered of the same shape as the sugar, either one $20.00. I know of no other pieces. *Not to be confused with Austrian.*

No. 2395 – FINE CUT MEDALLION – K. Bk. 2-37 – (Not pictured). Clear, non-flint of the early 90s. Very like Cane Medallion, the only differences being that the tall pieces are higher and the medallions are filled with fine cut instead of cane. Same values. *Better known as Grand. Bryce, Higbee, c 1885.*

No. 1777 – SPALDING – Mil. 105. Clear, non-flint of the 80s; goblet $15.00.

NEW FAKES OUT

Mrs. Kamm gave as one reason for collecting this late glass was the fact that it had not been reproduced. What a shock she would get, were she alive today. One scarcely picks up a home type magazine but she finds advertised some of it and to make matters worse, it's advertised as E.A.P.G. made from old molds. The latter part may be true, for it is so recent that many of the old molds are around in usable condition. Lately I saw Fancy Diamonds cracker jar so advertised and a set of six goblets containing Atlanta for one. Recently another set of older goblets is out with the old standbys and this includes Frosted Flower Band. One has to keep watching.

1886
Regal Block

1853
Block with
Sawtooth Band

1561
Alligator Scales

1560
Alligator Scales with
Spearpoint

1763
Pittsburgh Fan

1734
Pittman

2438
Ribs and Diamonds

1360
Chestnut

166

No. 1886 – REGAL BLOCK – Mil. Bk. 2-97. Clear, non-flint of the 80s; $15.00. *Cooperative Flint Glass Co., #190, c 1892.*

No. 1853 – BLOCK WITH SAWTOOTH BAND – Mil. 136. Clear, non-flint of the 90s; *goblet $20.00.*

No. 1561 – ALLIGATOR SCALES – Mil. Bk. 2-12. Clear, non-flint of the 70s. Goblet $30.00.

No. 1560 – ALLIGATOR SCALES WITH SPEAR POINT – Mil. Bk. 2-127. Clear, non-flint of the 70s; goblet $25.00.

No. 1763 – PITTSBURG FAN (Millard's spelling). Clear, non-flint of the 90s; *goblet $25.00.*

No. 1734 – PITTMAN – Mil. Bk. 2-20. Clear, non-flint of 1889. *Bellaire Goblet Co., #16; U.S. Glass, 1891. Goblet $25.00.*

No. 2438 – RIBS AND DIAMONDS – Mil. Bk. 2-101. Clear, non-flint of the 80s; *goblet $20.00.*

No. 1360 – CHESTNUT – M. 129. Clear amber, blue and I expect canary in non-flint of the 80s; same values making the usual allowance for color. Some of these goblets are trimmed with etching which detracts instead of adding to them but they can be found either way; it does not change value. *Westmoreland, #91, c 1898. Clear $20.00; blue $35.00; canary $45.00.*

GOOD DEALERS CAN HELP COMBAT SELLING INFERIOR MERCHANDISE AND FAKES

A couple of years ago, I went out to visit a rather large suburban show in which one of the dealers had some fake colored Wildflower. I believe he did not know so I said, "You had better not bring that to the _____ Show," one in which we were both going to show and which was a restricted show, "or I'll put up a howl." He didn't, but he brought a booth of carnival glass. Our clientele was choice. He met me at the end of the first day and inquired as to business. "Great!" I told him. His only answer was, "Horrors." He's dealing with the public in another line now.

I attended another show in which the dealer across from me had some of the same new fake colored Wildflower. He said he knew it was new and told people so but it was not so marked. I complained to the management, who were running the show as a benefit and knew nothing of the business. This year I had a letter from them asking me to come in and they said the dealer who displayed the new glass would not be let in again. So you see the right kind of dealer can help.

1363
Greek Cross Band

1872
Prince Albert

1603
Ring and Swirl

1651
Prism Flute with
Cog Band

2390
Double Snail

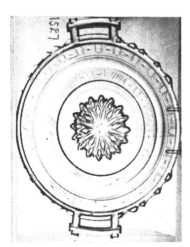

1527
Two Band

835
Heavy Basketweave
Open Floral Edge

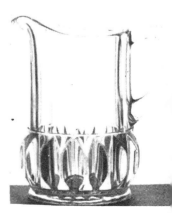

1623
Cordova

No. 1363 – GREEK CROSS – Mil. Bk. 2-162. Clear, flint of the late 60s. This is a surprising pattern to be found in flint glass, but surprises never end in this study. Flint goblet $40.00; if in non-flint $25.00.

No. 1368 – MALTESE CROSS – Mil. 35 – (Not pictured). At first glance, this goblet seems the same as the one above, the main difference is in the stem, which in this is plain, in the glass quality, which here is non-flint and a minor difference in the design of the squares. Then too, the bowl of Greek Cross is angular, while the bowl of this is rounded. Goblet $30.00.

No. 1872 – PRINCE ALBERT – Mil. 171. Clear and colored, non-flint of the 80s. Clear goblet $20.00. *Columbia Glass Co., c 1888.*

No. 1603 – RING AND SWIRL – Mil. Bk. 2-139. Clear, non-flint of the 80s. Spooner $15.00; sugar $10.00; creamer $18.00; covered butter $25.00; covered sugar $30.00; large cakestand $35.00. Dalzell, Gilmore & Leighton Co., c 1890.

No. 1651 – PRISM FLUTE WITH COG BAND – Mil. Bk. 2-96. Clear, non-flint of the late 80s. Goblet $20.00.

No. 1527 – TWO BAND – K. Bk. 1-64. Clear, non-flint of the late 80s and early 90s made in many forms including large handled plate shown here $18.00; *bowl $12.00.*

No. 835 – HEAVY BASKET WEAVE OPEN EDGE PLATE – L. 187 – Shown in my Booklet No. 4. This odd plate is a relative of the tall basketweave compote found in clear $25.00; blue $40.00; milk glass $30.00. The plate comes in clear $20.00; canary $60.00; amber $30.00; blue $40.00. *Aka Floral Fence.*

No. 2390 – DOUBLE SNAIL – K. Bk. 5-93. Clear, heavy, non-flint of the early 90s. Made by George Duncan & Sons of Pittsburgh. Four sizes of pitchers, small or large creamer, milk pitcher, water pitcher, rose bowl, shown. *Comes in 3", 5", 6", and 7". $45.00 – 70.00.*

No. 2389 – SNAIL – K. Bk. 2-69 – L.V. 46 calls it COMPACT, its original trade name. Made by Doyle and Co. of Pittsburgh and reissued by the U.S. Glass Co., probably in the early 90s. The pattern is very like Double Snail above only in this there is only one row of snails; sometimes they run to the right and at others to the left; on covered pieces they may alternate. Space above may be plain or etched; it does not change value. Salt shaker, each $20.00; 3", 5" rose bowls $45.00; 9" bowl $25.00; spooner $30.00; open sugar $20.00; sherbet cup $12.00; individual creamer $18.00; sugar shaker $60.00; celery $40.00; cruet $60.00; 9" cakestand $110.00; creamer $40.00; 6", 7" rose bowl $60.00; milk pitcher $35.00; covered butter, open compote, covered sugar $55.00; water pitcher $100.00; 10" cakestand $120.00; covered tall compote $125.00. Ruby 100% more.

No. 1623 – CORDOVA – L.V. 66 – K. Bk. 1-103. Clear, non-flint made in 1890 in many pieces, including vases; water pitcher shown $65.00. *O'Hara Glass, c 1891; U.S. Glass, 1904. Also found in emerald green, add 50%.* This pattern gave me an example of a dealer, who thought she had been in business many years was neither a student nor informed. As I entered her shop one day she greeted me with, "I've something fine to show you — a rare piece of Spanish glass," and she sallied forth to the rear quarter, to bring forth her treasure. Back she came with a piece of Cordova in her hand. Sounds Spanish, doesn't it?

1897
Diamond Splendor

1900
Spector Block

1890
Devon

1446
Roped Diamond

2048
Chesterfield

1459
Knotted Cord

1365
Crusader Cross

2047
Lace Checkerboard

No. 1897 – DIAMOND SPLENDOR – Mil. 40. Clear, and ruby stain non-flint of the 80s. *Aka All Over Diamond. Duncan #356, c 1890; U.S. Glass, c 1892. Ruby add 50%.*

No. 1900 – SPECTRE BLOCK – Mil. Bk. 2-78. Clear, non-flint of the same era. *Goblet $20.00.*

No. 1890 – DEVON – Mil. Bk. 2-45. Clear, non-flint of the 80s; same values.

No. 1446 – ROPED DIAMOND – Mil. Bk. 2-109. Clear, non-flint, same era $30.00.

No. 2048 – CHESTERFIELD – Mil. Bk. 2-74. Clear, non-flint of the 80s; $25.00. *Cambridge Glass #2500, c 1903.*

No. 1365 – CRUSADER CROSS – Mil. Bk. 2-44 – L.V. 44 calls it STAR and lists several pieces. Clear, non-flint of the 80s; $20.00.

No. 1459 – KNOTTED CORD – Mil. Bk. 2-102. Clear, non-flint of the 80s; $35.00.

No. 2047 – LACE CHECKERBOARD – Mil. Bk. 2-12 calls this Checkerboard but as there is another late pattern by that name I've added a word. Of the 80s, clear, non-flint. *Goblet $25.00.*

WHAT IS OLD GLASS?

When one is eight years old, a teenager is grown up to her and how she longs for the grown up estate of a teenager; when she becomes a teenager she hankers for the freedom of the mature twenties; when she is twenty she longs for the home owning, children raised peace of the forties that's where life begins — or does it; in other words, what is old, especially in glass?

When one is thirty-five or forty, she remembers only glass about fifteen or twenty years back and glass thirty to forty years is definitely old and fifty to sixty, "Why of course it's antique, I never saw anything like it." But after one's hair has turned to silver (or to be more realistic, an icky white) and the furrows have deepened, and she has seen innumerable collections in and out of museums, of glass which was well over one hundred years old, her ideas change with her hair and her skin. A teenager is an infant, forty years old (oh, well she'll learn better). So I find with the furrows deep, and the hair all white, I can't consider thirty, forty, fifty and at times sixty year old glass really old.

As ever there is a consolation. Recently, I celebrated a 90th birthday for a woman, a friend who is actively running a plumbing business. There are some old ones, young in character, and conversely, there are some young ones, old in good judgment; both are rare. The same is true of glass; there are a few late patterns of the 90s and even a very few years later, which have not taken on the normal exuberance and unrestrained loudness and boldness of the young, but which remain simple and restrained. They belong to the first families, the old families. Isn't it strange how human old glass is?

1771
Sheaf and Diamond

1774
Edgerton

1775
Fickle Block

1757
Split Diamond

1772
Antwerp

1766
Pan. Dia. Block

1762
Holbrook or
Cube with Dia.

1769
Block & Iris

No. 1771 – SHEAF AND DIAMONDS – Mil. 128. Clear, non-flint of the early 90s; $25.00. *Bryce, Higbee Co., c 1905; John Higbee 1907.*

No. 1774 – EDGERTON – Mil. Bk. 2-67. Clear, non-flint of the early 90s; same values as the others of this era.

No. 1775 – FICKLE BLOCK – Mil. Bk. 2-88 – K. Bk. 2-16 calls it SHEAF AND DIAMOND. Clear, non-flint, made in Pennsylvania in 1893, in four piece set and goblet and possibly more. Same value as the others of this period. *Aka Alden. Cooperative Flint Glass Co., c 1897.*

No. 1757 – SPLIT DIAMONDS – Heretofore unlisted; clear, non-flint of the late 80s or early 90s; same values as other members of the family. *Bellaire Goblet #17, c 1889; U.S. Glass, c 1891. Aka Triangles and Flute Fans.*

No. 1773 – ANTWERP – Mil. Bk. 2-8; shown in my Booklet No. 6. Clear, non-flint of the late 80s or early 90s, interesting stem. Goblet $25.00.

No. 1766 – PANELLED DIAMOND BLOCK – Mil. Bk. 2-146 – K. Bk. 6-42 and plate 56. Non-flint, clear or clear with colored top, made in 1894 by Duncan & Co. of Pennsylvania. This one definitely shows the influence of the imitation cut glass patterns which were flooding the market at this time and incidentally ruining the traditions of early American pattern glass. Spooner $15.00; open sugar $12.00; creamer $15.00; butter $20.00; goblet $20.00; covered sugar $20.00.

No. 1762 – HOLBROOK – Mil. Bk. 2-84 – L.V. 44 calls it CUBE WITH FAN – K. Bk. 3-79 calls it PINEAPPLE AND FAN. Clear, non-flint of the early 80s, very brilliant so it has quite a coterie of followers; made in many pieces. Sauce dish, flat $8.00; open sugar $12.00; tumbler $20.00; spooner $18.00; decanter $35.00; syrup $60.00; cruet $40.00; covered sugar $30.00; wine $25.00; goblet $30.00. *Adams & Co., later U.S. Glass, c 1895. The sugar without its lid is sometimes sold as a rose bowl because of its rounded shape and relatively small opening.*

WHAT GLASS DATA IS IMPORTANT?

As I've stated elsewhere, exact locale of manufacture and date cannot be given accurately. What then is important? The characteristics of certain eras which help us place a glass in that period. At first one might consider this impossible to do, but if you look at a page of the geometric blocks of the 80s and then compare them with the geometric block patterns of the 60s you will find a difference. In the 60s we do not find the small blocks, as glass becomes later we seem to find smaller units in the design, the design busier till it loses its character and in the imitation cut glass type which is not E.A.P.G. Later you will become like an artist who places artists in certain schools, such as the Hudson River School, etc., which means a definite kind of technique. Pattern glass divides itself into families which have much the same kind of characteristics. Later you will sense them. These are more evident when one sees the specimen rather than the pictures; that's why museum trips are important.

2208
Fine Cut Band

2201
Diamonds and
Cross Bars

1736
Diamond Prisms

1957
Cradled Prisms

473
Lobular Loops

2595
Perkins

2205
Isis

1411
Feather Duster—Huckel

174

No. 2208 – FINE CUT BAND – Mil. Bk. 2-153. Clear, non-flint, late 80s or early 90s; $20.00.

No. 2201 – DIAMONDS AND CROSSBARS – Mil. Bk. 2-13. Clear, non-flint of the mid 80s; $15.00.

No. 1736 – DIAMOND PRISMS – M. Bk. 2-25. Clear, non-flint of the 80s; *#1736 Albany preferred name. Tarentum Glass Co., c 1898. Aka Princeton. Goblet $35.00; cruet $40.00; ruby stain add 100%.*

No. 1957 – CRADLED PRISMS – K. Bk. 4-112. Clear, non-flint of the late 70s or early 80s. Creamer is footed. An interesting pattern; open sugar $15.00; spooner $30.00; covered butter $35.00; covered sugar $25.00; creamer $20.00. *Columbia Glass Co., 1885. Goblet $25.00.*

No. 473 – LOBULAR LOOPS – Mil. Bk. 2-148. Clear, non-flint of the 80s; same values as the others.

No. 2595 – PERKINS – Mil. 50. Clear, non-flint, imitation cut glass type. $25.00. *Higbee (Fashion) Glass, 1915; New Martinsville, 1918.*

No. 2205 – ISIS – Mil. Bk. 2-84. Clear, non-flint of the late 80s, has also been known as RADIANT D. & B. although it is not a member of that family. Same values as others of 1894. *McKee Bros., #132. Goblet $20.00; cakestand $35.00.*

No. 1411 – FEATHER DUSTER – K. Bk. 2-42 – L.V. 64 calls it ROSETTE MEDALLION. – Mil. Bk. 2-77 calls it HUCKEL. Small wonder collectors become confused. Clear and emerald green, of the mid 1900s. A "gold standard" campaign plate of William McKinley for the 1896 campaign has a border of this pattern. Values same as others of this era with the exception of the historical plate which is very popular and brings $200.00. The green is also liked and brings an additional 75%. *U.S. Glass, 1895.*

2154
Tennis Racquet

2159
Deflating Balloon

1422
Balloon

2603
Colonial with Garland

2537
Flamboyant

2598
Fern Burst
Two Views

2594
Feather Swirl

No. 2154 – TENNIS RACQUET – Mil. Bk. 2-97. Clear, non-flint of the late 80s or early 90s. Wine, goblet $25.00. *Aka Windsor. U.S. Glass #15102, c 1907.*

No. 2159 – DEFLATING BALLOON – Heretofore unlisted. Clear, non-flint of the late 80s. Goblet, wine (shown) $12.00.

No. 1422 – BALLOON – Mil. 107. Clear, thin, non-flint glass; really quite modern. Goblet, wine. Not E.A.P.G. *Sun Ray No. 2510 by Fostoria, 1935 – 1944.*

No. 2603 – COLONIAL WITH GARLAND – Mil. Bk. 2-111 – K. Bk. 4-106; base impresses, "Nu-cut," which definitely removes it from the realm of E.A.P.G. No. relative of the early colonial family. Wine $12.00; goblet $20.00.

No. 2537 – FLAMBOYANT – Mil. Bk. 2-83. Clear, non-flint of the imitation cut glass type and you know what I think of that; goblet $15.00; wine $10.00.

No. 2598 – FERNBURST – Mil. Bk. 2-67. Two views shown. Another of the imitation cut glass type. Enough said. Goblet $25.00; wine $15.00.

No. 2594 – FEATHER SWIRL – M. Bk. 2-153. Another of the imitation cut glass type. $15.00.

2602
Pecorah

2608
Gothic Arch

2606
Pan. Heather

2064
Bosworth or Star Band

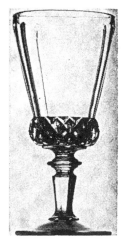

2601
Flute with Dia. Band

1720
U. S. Thumb.

2487
Yoke Band

2096
Despot

No. 2602 – PECORAH – Mil. 150. Clear, non-flint of the early 90s. Another of the late patterns which shows the influence of the imitation cut glass patterns flooding the market at this time. Goblet is the least offending in design of the pattern; sugars and creamers are awkward and clumsy and fussy and not E.A.P.G. Shown in my Booklet No. 6. Goblet $20.00.

No. 2608 – GOTHIC ARCH – Mil. Bk. 2-116; shown in my Booklet No. 2. Clear, non-flint of the 90s. Remainder of pattern, with the exception of the wine and the goblet, awkward, clumsy and beyond the pale. Wine $12.00; goblet $20.00.

No. 2606 – PANELLED HEATHER – Mil. 152; shown in my Booklet No. 5. Clear, non-flint of the early 90s; wine $10.00; goblet $25.00; cakestand $35.00; all fairly good design; the remainder, uninteresting. *Glass sometimes gray, not always clear.*

No. 2064 – BOSWORTH – Mil. Bk. 2-19 – K. Bk. 4-83 calls it STAR BAND, a name which she gives to a much earlier pattern in Bk. 1, so in this case, I believe it wiser to keep Millard's term. Shown in my Booklet No. 6. Worthless in all pieces except the goblet which is no great treasure $15.00. *Jenkins Glass, c 1910.*

No. 2601 – FLUTE WITH DIAMOND BAND – Mil. Bk. 2-90; shown in my Booklet No. 6. Clear, non-flint of the 90s and no relation to the early Flute family. Millard describes it as "very pretty," it may be that but it's in a modern way it has no characteristics of E.A.P.G. The other pieces in the setting were not noted for grace. Goblet $15.00.

No. 1720 – U.S. THUMBPRINT – K. Bk. 5-5. Shown in my Booklet No. 5. Clear, non-flint shown in the U.S. Glass Co. Catalog of 1892, but I feel it may be a reissue of a pattern of an earlier date as the simplicity of this pattern and good design of pieces seems to indicate that it belongs to late 70s or early 80s. Goblet shows interesting, related, co-ordinated detail in stem. Goblet $15.00; spooner $15.00; open sugar $8.00; creamer $12.00; covered butter $20.00; covered sugar $15.00.

No. 2487 – YOKE BAND-PLAIN STEM – Mil. Bk. 2-164. Thin, clear, non-flint of the early 90s. Quite modern in its feeling, goblet $20.00.

No. 2096 – DESPOT – Mil. Bk. 2-81. Clear, non-flint of the 90s; very modern in appearance; goblet $10.00.

NOTE: No matter how much Mrs. Metz praised simplicity of design, collectors today want glass that has the look and feel of an antique, not something plain and unadorned that looks modern, like Despot.

Another window of the Sandwich Museum. Loan collection or Diamond Point belong to Miss Jane Wakefield.

MUSEUMS OF SPECIAL INTEREST TO PATTERN GLASS COLLECTORS

There are many fine museums in our country, but I feed that E.A.P.G. collectors will find the following a joy to visit. Not all of them are open all year round or all days of the week so I suggest you write to them for information before you plan your trip. Take more than one trip to them — visit a while, have your book with you, go to your room, leaf through your book. An ideal way is to spend time in the museum, spend the evening checking through one's book and noting questions to yourself, return the next day and check the things you want to answer. Don't hurry, you'll regret it later.

First and foremost is the Sandwich Museum, located at Sandwich, Massachusetts, near the sites of both the Sandwich and the New England Glass Co., two of our finest companies. A beautiful old town, with its unpretentious building among grand old trees, proudly guarding and displaying in an American way one of our fine heritages. There is other glass besides pattern, lacy Sandwich, free blown, and much on glassmaking history, showing molds, etc. The cases and windows are a joy. Mrs. Doris Kershaw, the curator, is a niece of Nicholas Lutz, one of our early glassmakers. If you haven't been there since the new wing was added, you should go back. Open from May till October.

Portland Art Museum, Portland, Maine. I believe more Portland glass than is to be found anyplace. Beautifully displayed. Many of our pictures are from there.

Bennington Museum, Bennington, Vermont. A collection of 1,250 goblets. Here also is a collection of fakes displayed next to the genuine ones. Although art glass is not my line, I've never seen it displayed as tastefully and intelligently as it is here. It is all labeled as to kind. As an added treat to pattern glass lovers there are two pieces displayed under a dome on a table; they are so unusual it is almost hard to believe they are real. One is a handled goblet in Lattice and Oval Panel, engraved "Forget me not." The other is a handled egg cup in Gothic. Where these one of a kind articles come from, I'd never know. Mr. Richard Barrett is the curator of Bennington Museum and has always been recognized as an authority in this field, but when you visit the museum, you will see he knows many other lines thoroughly. In content, manner of display and labeling, this museum is outstanding.

Allen Art Museum, Oberlin College, Oberlin, Ohio. Dr. Bruce Swift's collection of 1,500 goblets.

Judy's Museum, Mountain View, Missouri, has a room full of good pattern glass plus other interesting rooms. This was collected by Dr. Grace Doane of Des Moines, Iowa.

The Willard Mellvilles of Colgate, Wisconsin, have quite an extensive collection of goblets for people to see.

The Edison Museum at Milan, Ohio, has a large room of glass.

Other notable glass museums not listed by Mrs. Metz:
Greentown Glass Museum
Greentown, IN
Extensive displays of Greentown Glass
(Indiana Tumbler and Goblet)

Jones Gallery of Glass & Ceramics
Douglas Hill, ME
Over 7,000 pieces of glass and ceramics from ancient to modern

Henry Ford Museum & Greenfield Village
Dearborn, MI
A large collection of pressed glass is displayed and arranged in chronological and functional order, such as tableware, decorative, lighting, bottles, and containers.

Wheaton Museum of American Glass
Millville, NJ
Largest museum in U.S. devoted to American glass

Corning Museum of Glass
Corning Glass Center, Corning, NY
Contains world's most comprehensive collection of glass. It is the largest in the United States devoted exclusively to glass.

Houston Antique Museum
Chattanooga, TN
Extensive collection of glass pitchers

Mansion Museum of Oglebay Institute
Oglebay Park, Wheeling, WV
Displays of glass produced in the area

Fenton Glass Museum
Williamstown, WV
In addition to a working glass factory, there is a comprehensive museum of the company's glass.

1203
McKinley Campaign Plate

1297
McKinley Memorial Plate

1206
Sheridan Memorial Plate

1225
Pope Leo **Plate**

1227
Train Platter

1204
Columbus **Plate**

1462
Picket or Reaper Tray

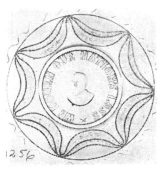

1256
Garfield Drape Plate

1189
Niagara Falls Tray

No. 1203 – McKINLEY CAMPAIGN PLATE – Large, clear plate, put out in 1895, the year of presidential campaign of William McKinley; value $55.00.

No. 1297 – McKINLEY MEMORIAL TRAY – Small sized tray, put out after his assassination in 1901. Inscription, "It is God's way," at top, "His will be done," at the bottom, date of birth and death at sides of figure. Value $75.00.

No. 1206 – SHERIDAN MEMORIAL PLATE – A plate honoring the Civil War hero, probably issued after his death in 1888. Clear only, value $75.00.

No. 1225 – POPE LEO – The plate is of Pope Leo, the thirteenth, who reigned from 1878 to 1903 and whose brilliant and holy pontificate left many important documents including those on the important topic of the day, Capital and Labor Relations. His fame had spread to such proportions that this plate was issued commercially, not as a church souvenir, plate in clear only, value $40.00. I do not know when the plate was put out, most likely at his death.

No. 1227 – RAILROAD TRAIN PLATTER – This one is in the Sandwich Museum. This platter was made by Bakewell Pears of Pittsburgh, Pennsylvania, in 1882. Scarce, value $125.00. Reproduced, new is heavier, stippling not fine.

No. 1204 – COLUMBUS-THE NAVIGATOR – I believe this plate came out in 1892. Clear only, value $50.00.

No. 1462 – PICKET PLATTER – Also known as REAPER BREAD TRAY – The pickets are further apart than they are in other pieces of the well known Picket pattern but platters sometimes vary. Clear only. Scarce, value $125.00. From the Willard Melville collection.

No. 1256 – GARFIELD DRAPE MEMORIAL PLATTER – Put out after the president's assassination in the well known pattern, Garfield Drape. Value $55.00.

No. 1189 – NIAGARA FALLS TRAY – Probably produced in 1885 after the Canadian Park was completed and the New York reservation was opened. Large, heavy, clear and frosted tray with fine detail showing Prospect Point at the Falls and even the Maid of the Mist plies her way below. Value $175.00.

1163
Dewey Pitcher

1164
Gridley Pitcher

1200
Grant & Wilson

1060
Jumbo and Barnum

8
Girl of
Lily

2600
Nellie Blye Tray

1197
Gibson Girl

1230
Rock of Ages

No. 1163 – DEWEY PATTERN – K. Bk. 2-123 calls it SPANISH-AMERICAN, because she uses this title here for the pattern Flower Flange. This was, of course, a memento of that war. The other side of the popular water pitcher shows the head of the admiral, encircled in a wreath. It was around for many years, must have been made in great quantities, was even given as baking powder premiums. The matching tumbler is much scarcer than the water pitcher, which is being greatly over priced by some today; pitcher or tumbler $50.00 – 60.00; clear only. Put out on about the last years of the 90s; shown in my Booklet No. 5. *Not part of the Greentown Dewey pattern.*

No. 1164 – GRIDLEY PITCHER – K. Bk. 5-135. Contemporary of above. If you have trouble distinguishing the two, it is easy to remember that the Dewey has a border of cannon balls, while the Gridley has the border of shells. The Gridley pitcher is scarcer than the Dewey, but is not as well known, so there is not the demand and the price is about the same. I've never seen a Gridley tumbler but there should be one. *$50.00 – 60.00.*

No. 1200 – GRANT AND WILSON GOBLET – Listed but not pictured in my first book. Goblet now $600.00. *From presidential campaign of 1872. Greely & Brown, opposing candidates.*

No. 1060 – JUMBO AND BARNUM – Listed and described in my first book but not pictured. Prices not, spooner $150.00; creamer $125.00; covered sugar $550.00; covered butter $475.00; *spoon rack $900.00; in blue $1,800.00.*

No. 8 – GIRL OF LILY – Listed for the first time in my Booklet No. 1. This sugar was sent to me by Mr. Wisecarver of Pennsylvania and it is a rarity. Of very early flint this specimen is grayed. I've heard it has been called EVE and LITTLE EVA. It was probably made in the fifties and was part of a set. If clear glass $150.00; grayed specimen $110.00.

No. 2600 – NELLIE BLYE TRAY – Clear, commemorative tray issued as the famous Nellie Blye, established a record as the first woman to travel around the world alone. Her time is on the tray, "Around the world in 72D'S, 6H's, 11M's." A scarce item; I was searching for one for the old Chicago luggage firm which had made the little reticule which she carries in her hand and which still has the pattern of it. It took me two years to find it. Shown in my Booklet No. 2; the tray was made in Pennsylvania in the 90s, her trip was completed January 1890. Value $200.00. *Often found with damage.*

No. 1197 – GIBSON GIRL – K. Bk. 2-26. Clear, non-flint of the early 1900s. Here is an example of a very late glass which has the character and worth with qualities of a much earlier period and proves we can't go by the calendar alone in judging merit of glass. This tells us of its era; we know how the Gibson Girl looks, for here she is, black velvet bow, pompadour and all; it has a story and tells it well. I've seen a tumbler so there probably is a water pitcher. Creamer $75.00; tumbler $65.00; water pitcher $135.00.

No. 1230 – ROCK OF AGES PLATTER – Bears the patent mark "Dec. 7, 1875." Another, "Give us this day our daily bread," and a rather scarce one. Clear only. This one belongs to the Willard Melvilles of Wisconsin. Value $100.00; with milk glass center $145.00.

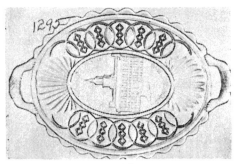

1295
Washington Centennial Platter

1296
Prescott and Stark

1290
Continental Platter

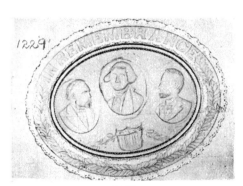

1229
In Remembrance Platter

1293
Campaign Plate

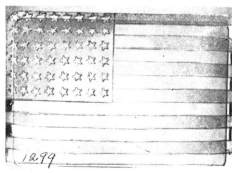

1299
Flag Tray

No. 1295 – WASHINGTON CENTENNIAL PLATTER – Listed, but not pictured in my first book. The inscription at the top reads, "Our nation's birthplace," and at the bottom, "Independence Hall." Value now $135.00. *Part of Washington pattern.*

No. 1296 – PRESCOTT AND STARK-THE HEROES OF BUNKER HILL – One of a series of historical plates made by Gillinder and Co. for the Centennial Exposition at Philadelphia in 1876. Clear only, value $120.00.

No. 1290 – CONTINENTAL PLATE – Another of this series of historical plates sold at the Philadelphia Exposition; clear only, value $85.00.

No. 1229 – IN REMEMBRANCE PLATTER – A memorial platter, issued after Garfield's assassination in 1881; Garfield is given a place with Lincoln and Washington. Clear only, value $75.00. *Reproduced.*

No. 1293 – CAMPAIGN PLATES – Made in clear by Gillinder and Co. of Pittsburgh, Pennsylvania, for the hot presidential campaign of 1884 and the next campaign in 1888. P. Jacobus, the greatest moldmaker of all, was the sculptor of these figure molds; and they are considered about the finest specimen of the mold maker's art from the technical point of view. The plate shown with the ivy border came with Blain and Logan, Cleveland and Hendricks and for the following campaign, Harrison and Morton and Cleveland and Thurman. Any of these trays now $195.00; the classic plate with Blaine or Logan is $225.00. All are only in clear.

No. 1299 – FLAG TRAY – There was a flag tray made for the Centennial and it had thirty eight stars for the states then in existence. The tray shown could not have been made prior to 1912, according to the number of its stars. The older flag tray has a plain border, value $300.00; later flag tray $275.00. Both clear. *Reproduced.*

Tray

Mug

1263
Knights of Labor

1236
Royal Lady Compote

1233
Faith, Hope and Charity

1236
Royal Lady Cheese Dish—Base

1231
Late Eagle Plate

1213
Garfield Plate

No. 1263 – KNIGHTS OF LABOR PLATTER – Made by Bakewell Pear of Pittsburgh in 1879. Clear and colors, non-flint; value canary $250.00; tumbler $175.00; blue $200.00; clear $125.00.

No. 1263 – KNIGHTS OF LABOR MUGS – Only clear has been seen in the mugs, probably, made at the same time by the same firm as the platter. Besides the one shown, there is another, very alike in shape, which shows the workman shaking hands with a bearded, frock coated, old gentleman; it bears the legend, "Arbitration." Value of either mug $75.00. *Mug found in three sizes.*

No. 1236 – ROYAL LADY – K. Bk. 4 calls it simply ROYAL, but there is another pattern by that name, so I've added. Compote shown and cheese dish. Clear, non-flint, made by Belmont Glass Co. in Bellaire, Ohio, in the early 80s. The creamer and sugar have short legs ending in little balls. Compote shown $75.00; creamer $35.00; covered sugar $45.00; cheese dish $85.00. The base to the cheese dish would be difficult to identify if one did not recognize these little tabs as a unit of the pattern.

No. 1213 – GARFIELD PLATE – This plate is frequently described as having 101 border; this border is really what is called egg and dart in design and the pattern 101 has an entirely different border. The center is Garfield. It is clear, non-flint of the 80s; value $75.00.

No. 1233 – FAITH, HOPE AND CHARITY PLATE – Also known as THE THREE GRACES. Clear, non-flint of the 80s; plate $60.00.

No. 1231 – LATE EAGLE PLATE – This plate came out in *1942* and does not look old, does not belong with old glass, but there are those who collect things with eagles. It is shown here for their information. *Made during 1942, plate $15.00; footed sherbet $12.00; cup $15.00; tumbler $35.00.*

870
Magnet and Grape
Frosted Leaf Jug

74
Washington Head Butter

74
Rectangular Covered Bowl

275
Ribbed Ivy
Decanter—
Original Stopper

1917
Ribbon Rectangular Dolphin
Stemmed Compote

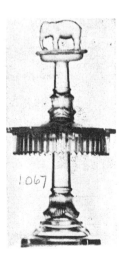

1067
Jumbo Spoon Rack

PATTERN GLASS RARITIES

No. 870 – MAGNET AND GRAPE WITH FROSTED LEAF WINE JUG – From the Sandwich Museum. It's hard to value this type of thing. The way some art glass is going I'd say it was worth it, ex. rare $1,200.00 – 1,500.00.

No. 74 – HORN OF PLENTY RECTANGULAR BOWL – From Sandwich Museum. 6½" x 4" x 5½" to top of cover. Another unique piece that is apt to bring almost anything and I believe it should. *One with undertray sold for $12,000.00 in 1998. Considered a sugar casket.*

No. 74 – HORN OF PLENTY WASHINGTON HEAD BUTTER – From the Sandwich Museum. Not quite as rare as bowl above but just try and find one. Value $950.00.

No. 275 – RIBBED IVY DECANTER WITH ORIGINAL STOPPER – From the Sandwich Museum. Value $350.00; without stopper $250.00.

No. 1917 – RIBBON RECTANGULAR DOLPHIN STEM COMPOTE – A scarce member of this family, also is found in the round. Value $225.00. *Reproduced in colors, new does not have wafer attaching top to base.*

No. 1067 – JUMBO SPOON RACK – Since this has been listed as a rarity, more have appeared, as frequently happens. The goblet is as rare; value $600.00.

THE PRICES OF OLD GLASS
WHY PRICE LISTS?

I'd like to stress that prices I list are suggested areas of value and not hard and fast dollars and cents valuations, covering all sections of our country. Please do not tell a dealer that she is so much higher than I list, especially if you are on the far west, or if you are looking at an old edition of my book and have not changed prices according to new formula on front pages of my later editions. Price seems only factor in minds of many; this was proven to me after I issued my booklets. There was five times the demand of Booklet No. 1 with the price list of all the goblets than for any other. Price must be judged on many factors.

What are the factors determining a dealer's asking price? What he has to pay, I hear you reply. But think of the things involved in that cost. Just last fall I had my car heater repaired, when bill came in, it stated parts $7.00; labor $16.00. I thought of our line. Many times when we are called to buy a collection the owner thinks we merchandise at 25% mark up. She does not figure, insurance, advertising costs, travel costs, etc. I tell them of the car heater and that we, too, have overhead and expenses, even Social Security tax for our help. If glass is not clean many imperfections cannot be seen, and what one thinks is a bargain is not. It takes help to maintain stock.

What are some of the factors influencing the fluctuating of some of the prices of some of the patterns and some of the pieces? In some cases the answer is demand caused by a legitimate style trend, such as the counter wash basin, which is using compotes and sometimes it is speculation such as is happening in Indiana Glass and some patterns such as Grasshopper and Klondyke.

The number of collectors has grown by leaps and bounds, and a legitimate rise is normal but speculative prices are not, and the only way to combat them is to ignore pieces in which it is prevalent.

1095
Lion Egg Cup

63
Bull's Eye with
Fleur-de-lys Celery

1544
Shell and Tassel—Oyster Plate

1544
Vase

122
Argus Pickle Jar

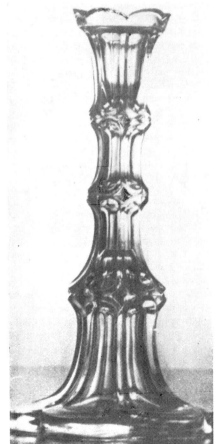

113
Excelsior
Candlestick

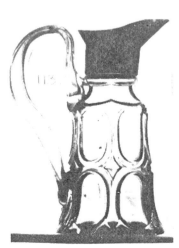

Syrup

812
Holly Covered Compote

No. 113 – EXCELSIOR SYRUP – Scarce syrup in the fine old pattern; value $175.00. From the Nickerson collection on Cape Cod. Hollow, blown applied handle; a remarkable example of early glass, a unique specimen has been found in moss green from the Wakefield collection; value $850.00.

No. 113 – EXCELSIOR CANDLESTICK – L. 34. Mrs. Lee stated that this was the first pattern which had a candle-stick. Single $120.00; pair $350.00 – 400.00.

No. 63 – BULL'S EYE WITH FLEUR DE LIS – For some unknown reason the celery of this fine early flint is very diffi-cult to find; value $300.00.

No. 1544 – SHELL AND TASSEL VASE – From the Sandwich Museum. Although goblet has been reproduced, I've seen no other reproduction in this pattern. Vase $140.00.

No. 1544 – SHELL AND TASSEL OYSTER PLATE – From the Sandwich Museum. Had anyone told me she had seen this I'd have concluded she had been dreaming. But here it is; I've never seen it listed, never heard of anyone who had seen it. Why does a loner appear? I know not. This is the never ending surprise of collecting. Value $295.00.

No. 1095 – LION EGG CUP – In this pattern one has to constantly watch for reproductions. Value $95.00. Other scarce items are the collared base, oval master salt $200.00; and the cologne bottle, unique $350.00. Neither of the last two have been reproduced so far.

No. 122 – ARGUS PICKLE JAR – Hitherto unlisted. We find these jars in a few of the early patterns, although this is the first time this has appeared, value $250.00.

No. 812 – HOLLY COVERED COMPOTE – This delightful pattern is all hard to find and the 8" covered com-pote is really a find. Value $295.00.

All of the above patterns are listed in my first book, but these rarities are not and they are important.

BEWARE OF

The alibi — "I got this in an old home." It means absolute-ly nothing. Grandma may have seen a fake in the gift shop that reminded her of childhood in her old home and brought it. The auctioneer's statement — Many catalogs state that they are not responsible for the statement of their auctioneer. Few have experts to check the collection. Country auctions are sometimes stuffed deliberately.

Believing that because a dish is chipped, had bubbles or is slightly crooked that it is old.

Believing that because a piece varies in slight detail from one you possess it is not old.

The "selling out sale." As George Gobel, posing as a busi-nessman, said, when queried as to occupation, "Selling out sales."

1917—Dresser Set in Ribbon

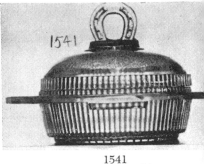

1541
Snowdrop Covered Butter

1460—Cord & Tassel

1181
Actress—Two Drominos Cheese Dish

1268
Good Luck Cheese Dish

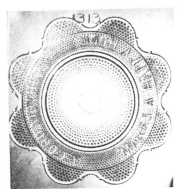

1313—Star Rosette
Good Mother Plate

1822—Hand Mug

2019—Loop and Dart
Wooden Base Butter

No. 1917 – DRESSER SET IN RIBBON – A rarity in this fine pattern. Three piece set $175.00; pair of bottles $95.00; note stoppers are not frosted; pomade jar $60.00; cover is not frosted. The wine in this pattern is now in the scarce stage and is worth $125.00; in goblets, one must watch for reproductions. Shown in my Booklet No. 3. *Ribbons were frosted by grinding and are rough to the touch.*

No. 1181 – THE TWO DROMINOS–ACTRESS CHEESE DISH – Again we see a cheese dish differing from the pattern, but the long medallions are there. This is in the collections of the Melvilles of Wisconsin. Value $350.00.

No. 1541 – SNOWDROP – Millard calls this lovely pattern ASHLAND. This attractive butter dish is in the Portland Museum. Value $85.00. *From the angle shown, one cannot see the shape. Appears to be Horseshoe.*

No. 2019 – LOOP AND DART BUTTER-WOODEN BASE – One of the loveliest pieces I've seen, the base is beautifully carved in hard wood. I never believed such a thing existed until I saw this in the Portland Museum. One has to see this to enjoy it fully. Value $95.00. *Probably a "make do" carved to replace a broken glass base. Not a production item, but collectible to many.*

No. 1268 – GOOD LUCK-HORSESHOE CHEESE DISH – Base also shown. Shown in my Booklet No. 4. I bought this from a dealer who does not believe in "book learning," and who sold it to me, as Loop and Dart. It is rarity of the pattern. Value $395.00.

No. 1313 – STAR ROSETTED-GOOD MOTHER PLATE – Fast becoming rare. Its motto, "A good mother makes a happy home," has made it too suitable for gifts for it to remain on the market long. Value $50.00. *Many seen. Repro?*

No. 1460 – CORD AND TASSEL HANDLED MUG – From the Sandwich Museum. Hitherto unlisted. Mugs are getting hard to find in well known patterns and this one is scarce. Value $85.00. *Applied handle to tumbler.*

No. 1822 – HAND HANDLED MUG – Previously unlisted, from the Sandwich Museum. I have also found a cordial in this pattern, slightly larger than some cordials but a true cordial. Value hand mug $55.00; hand cordial $45.00. *Applied handle to tumbler.*

As one sees the listings in this book, it is easy to see why I say a serious student of E.A.P.G. should visit the Sandwich Museum. You'll never forget it.

All of the patterns listed on this page are listed in my Book 1.

Note: Applied handles are especially fragile at the bottom. Buyers should examine the fold of glass carefully for cracks. There is no such thing as a "heat check" that ever left the factories. A crack is damage and drastically reduces the value of the piece.

1457
Coolidge

521
Fine Rib and Star Lamp

1191
Stars and Stripes—
Night Light—
Two Views

845
Round Panelled Wheat Lamp

530
Double Handled Lamp

1357
Dotted American Shield Lamp

No. 1457 – COOLIDGE DRAPE LAMP – Clear, non-flint of the 80s, so named because this was the pattern of the lamp which stood on the table and lit the room in which President Coolidge took the oath of office at his grandfather's farm after President Harding's sudden death. Every now and then, I see it advertised as Lincoln Drape; in fact when I was looking for one for this picture I scanned the ads for one which showed by the remainder of the ad that the dealer did not know his glass and I found it and this lamp, incorrectly listed. This drape comes in several sizes, in clear and cobalt blue. Value of any size in clear $100.00; in cobalt blue $160.00.

No. 521 – FINE RIB AND STAR – Small clear glass, early flint of the 60s, but a kerosene lamp. These lamps with ivy vines make a pretty decorative note, value $125.00.

No. 1191 – STARS AND STRIPES-NIGHT LIGHT – Clear, non-flint, made by Safety Night Light Co. of Brooklyn, N.Y. It is really a container for a heavy candle; judging from the period of the kind of type on the lettering on the lamp, and the kind of glass, I'd say it was a product of the 80s. A collector's piece for lighting specialists. Value $95.00.

No. 845 – ROUND PANELLED WHEAT – Listed, but not pictured in my first book. Many patterns have their lamps; this one is especially appealing; value $120.00.

No. 530 – DOUBLE HANDLED LAMP – Interesting, clear, non-flint, double handled, kerosene lamp, bearing a patent of 1874. Value $150.00.

No. 1357 – DOTTED AMERICAN SHIELD – Another clear, non-flint kerosene, glass lamp of the 70s. Applied handle; value $175.00. *Reproduced.*

NOTE: For sperm oil lamps see pages near fore part of early flint patterns.

IMPROVING MAIL SERVICE — BOTH DEALERS AND COLLECTORS CAN HELP

Pattern glass is becoming so scarce that one must rely on mail buying to complete collections. To do this with the utmost profit to both parties, buying and selling procedures of both should be carefully examined. Both dealer and collector must have reference books and use the correct name of the pattern which he wishes. In sending a want to a dealer, the want should include not only the pattern name, but the size, if the dish comes as do sauce dishes in varied widths, number wanted and what pieces are wanted and what condition customer will accept. In his ad, dealer should carefully list name and give exact description of pattern and if errs, should pay transportation both ways. Otherwise, he should not accept merchandise returned. A collector can do much to keep prices down; unnecessary correspondence costs a dealer money; his helper may have to wait at post office to get a blank for C.O.D. order and then wait in line again to turn it in, his salary goes on. If a dealer does not have your want there is nothing gained by his answering and saying he has not. Anticipate your gifts; special handling, air mail all mean more time at post office windows; around holidays this can be especially rugged. I'm certain all dealers want to be courteous, but it is one field in which supervision of all individual orders generally has to be by the owners or owner. If it is one as in my case this is difficult.

897
Ramsay Grape

1532
Pleated Bands

2011
Pins and Bells

1670
Double Greek Key

608
Dewdrops
With Flowers
Quantico

CANADIAN GLASS

1094
Beaver Band

522
Bar and Finecut

802
Maple Wreath

CANADIAN GLASS

About two years ago, one of the most enjoyable experiences of my entire antique business and writing career, taught me what big mistakes authoritative writers could make in their own field, and this included me. At a time when the relations between our country and Canada were slightly strained, I was invited there to open a Toronto antique show. Press and public gave me a most warm and hearty welcome, but alas was my face red when I learned that several of the patterns which we Americans listed as ours were made there; another field to explore, more trips among these friendly, gracious people. From what I learned I have no doubt that some of the molds were made here for we exported molds to other countries. Many, many Canadians collect our glass, my publications have had a wide circulation there, had been reviewed on the air and in the press, unknown to me, until I reached there. It is an inspiring example of the "good neighbor" policy.

No. 1532 – PLEATED BANDS – Listed in my first book as American as did Mrs. Kamm before me. It was made by the Diamond Glass Co. (Lamont Glass Co.) of Nova Scotia in the 90s. I saw a cheese dish in this pattern in the Royal Museum in Toronto engraved with the name of one of the families connected with the firm. Plain cheese dish value $175.00.

No. 897 – RAMSAY GRAPE – Another pattern of the same period as the one above and made by the same firm. Listed by Millard and me in Book 1 as American. Made in complete set. I should not be surprised if this pattern had been made here also for I've seen it in two varying qualities, the Canadian is clear and bright with good detail $35.00; the other is cheap glass $20.00.

No. 608 – QUANTICO – Listed in my first book as American as did Dr. Millard. Canadian in full set. Goblet $40.00; open sugar $20.00; butter $75.00; celery $35.00; covered sugar $45.00; compote, covered $50.00; creamer $30.00.

No. 2011 – PINS AND BELLS – K. Bk. 4-8 lists this as American. As I entered the hall of the Hon. John Yaremko, an official of government in Canada, to see his glass, I glanced on the table in the next room where there was an entire collection of what I thought was Horseshoe, but when I got near to it, I saw it was Pins and Bells. Same values as Quantico above; made by the Humphrey Glass Works, in the 90s, in Nova Scotia, Canada.

No. 1670 – DOUBLE GREEK KEY – L.V. 38. Clear and stippled and opaque white, probably of the 80s made by Burlington Glass Works, Hamilton, Ontario, Canada, and in sets. Spooner $30.00; open sugar $15.00; covered butter $75.00; water tumbler $35.00; 6" tassi (shown) $30.00; covered sugar $45.00; covered compote $65.00; opalescent blue 250% additional.

No. 1094 – BEAVER BAND – Mil. Bk. 2-130. On the under side of the base is inscribed "St. Jean Baptiste-Quebec-24-June-1880." Made by Excelsior Glass Co. of St. John's, P.Q. just prior to the date on the bottom. I don't know whether this date marks the founding or the celebration of some anniversary of this society of which we have been hearing of late; they are working for the separation of the province of Quebec from the remainder of Canada. Value of goblet $1,200.00 – 1,500.00, as it is much sought after by collectors.

No. 522 – BAR AND FINECUT – Mil. Bk. 2-130 – Canadian. Note the very fancy stem detail, definitely a Canadian characteristic. Complete setting. Same values as Quantico. *Cake stand, square, $65.00.*

No. 802 – MAPLE WREATH – Shown in my Booklet No. 4. In Canada I saw the four piece set in clear and a lovely green, and also a beautiful milk glass butter dish. The maple leaf is so like the one in Beaver Band that I believe this to have been made by the same factory in the early 80s. Clear, spooner, open sugar $25.00; covered butter $85.00; creamer $35.00; covered sugar $45.00; in green or milk glass 60% additional.

I discovered other interesting things about patterns made in the adjoining countries. In my Book One, I said the Shell and Jewel had an extra row of balls so in Book Two here I show another picture; the Shell and Jewel shown in Book 1 is Canadian; Reverse Torpedo is Canadian. They made lamps, milk glass, canes, novelties, blown glass, lamp chimneys, glass chains, etc. Much more work can be done here.

No. 1

No. 2

Egyptian Glass

No. 3

No. 4

No. 5

VARIATIONS TO NOTE – COMPARISONS

No. 1 and 2 – Note variations on stippling of columns in these two; note profile of face, of figure, especially the nose.

No. 2 and 3 – Note clarity of band of small circles on pillar on 4 but notice differing facial profile of these two.

No. 3 and 4 – Note entire absence of band of small circles on band on pillar on 4 but notice differing facial profile of these two.

No. 4 and 5 – Note 5 has only nine well formed leaves on palm tree; 3 has ten; 2 has eleven. One can find many more, such as the little shrub which is almost missing at base of pillar in No. 5.

Possibly the foregoing will tend to show how carefully the real student of pattern glass must work.

VARIATIONS IN EGYPTIAN PATTERN GLASS

By Harold Allen

AUTHOR'S NOTE: I inserted this article by Mr. Harold Allen, who has been so much help with our photography to show you how carefully and thoughtfully he collects. He realizes these were not fakes; he's helped in more ways than in pictures. A.H.M.

With hundreds of patterns to choose from, every pressed glass collector must decide on some limits for his collection. A practical person may assemble one pattern in settings for its undeniable beauty and use on the table, while a rabid "collector" may want only one example of each piece in a set or in several sets. A third enthusiast may gather only one particular piece from many patterns, as Mrs. Kamm did so brilliantly with her pitchers. A fourth approach, and one favored by museums where display and storage are prime considerations, is to acquire only the showiest pieces from a number of outstanding sets. These four approaches pretty nearly comprised the ways to collect pattern glass until I stumbled on a fifth: I collect mold variations.

My pattern is Egyptian, a set made in the late 1870s and early eighties. At first, I tried to assemble it in place settings, but, as my collection grew, I noticed that not all the goblets were identical — nor all the compotes, sauces, spooners, sugar bowls, creamers, and butter and pickle dishes. The suspicion that some of these variants might be modern reproductions was dispelled by the very number of the deviations; why should so many pieces in a set that has never been more than moderate in price and popularity be reproduced as many as six or seven times? (I have six Egyptian goblets, all from different molds, and seven different Egyptian footed sauces, all the same size.) Moreover, dealers and students of glass, whose business it is to know about reproductions, assured me, and still assure me, that Egyptian has never been reproduced and that all the pieces are old.

Some minor variations can be explained by the repair or replacement of damaged or wornout molds. I have, for example, two goblets exactly alike except that one has an extra ridge on its foot. In this case apparently only part of a mold was changed and the rest reused, so I do not count this as a mold variation. The Cleopatra bread plate too shows signs of wear or damage on the mold. In some examples — apparently later impressions made after some alteration to the mold — the distant scene of the sphinx and palm trees is almost smoothed off, while in other, apparently earlier, impressions this scene is sharply detailed. Yet both types were pressed in the same mold.

It is possible that the original demand for Egyptian forced its manufacturer to duplicate molds for some of the pieces. A table setting would normally include several goblets and sauces for each spooner, sugar bowl, creamer, and butter dish, and this ratio is reflected in the number of variants I have found, which is highest in goblets and footed sauces. But this does not explain why there is an unusually high number of variation in butter dishes.

Duplications, repair, and replacements within a single factory can hardly account for the surprising number of variants in some pieces or for the equally surprising differences between variations — differences of quality as well as obviously intentional design changes. Some pieces were clearly not designed with the same taste or executed with the same skill as other versions of the same pieces. So it seems likely that at least some variations must be the products of more than one factory; probably several factories were producing Egyptian at roughly the same time.

Apparently not all pieces in the Egyptian set have variations. In the following I have never found evidence of more than one mold: water pitcher, celery vase, Cleopatra bread plate, 10" plate with handles, 8" flat serving bowl, 8" low compote, and 5" high compote. There are at least two versions each in the 7" flat serving bowl, 7" low compote, 7" high compote, 8" high compote, 4" footed sauce, and 3½" footed sauce. I have three variations each in the covered sugar bowl, spooner, creamer, 4" flat sauce, and 4½" pickle dish — but four variants in the 5½" pickle dish.

(Continued on page 203)

2714

Mug

Child's Creamer

823
Grape Line with Ovals

Tom Thumb
Mug

2714

1085

2715

Fighting Cats
Mug

Feeding Deer

Mug

1085

2715

I have five Egyptian butter dishes, all from different molds. Since the sphinx scene in the butter base is one of the easiest to compare, we are illustrating all five here. (I have seen a sixth Egyptian butter dish, different from all these five, but it is not available for a photograph). Three of my butter dishes have covers with sturdy rims, but on the other two the covers were made completely rimless. In spite of this all the covers are the same diameter, and all the covers fit all the bases!

On four of the footed pieces in the Egyptian set — the goblet, spooner, creamer, and sugar bowl–there may be either of two types of transition between the body and the stem. On some pieces this part is convex, or rounded outward; on the others it is concave, or hollowed. Convex pieces have the words RUINS OF PARTHENON below the temple scene, but many concave pieces omit this. I have never found evidence of more than one mold for the convex type, which is higher in quality and appears to be scarcer. In the concave type, however, I have two each of spooners, creamers, and sugar bowls — and five goblets, making the total variations in these four pieces 3, 3, 3, and 6.

My totals should not be considered final, since they represent only what I happen to have found thus far. Surely similar differences must exist in many other sets, and it would be good if we could tell the old variations from the modern reproductions. Last summer in an Iowa shop, I found four Westward Ho footed sauces, identical in size yet all obviously from different molds. In a coveted pattern such as Westward Ho, which we know has been reproduced repeatedly, one naturally assumes that at least three — possibly four — of the sauces were fakes. But, after the wild deviations, I have found in Egyptian — I wonder.

Note: Mr. Allen's collection was donated to the Chicago Art Institute upon his death about 1997.

No. 823 – GRAPE VINE WITH OVALS MUG – A children's novelty of the 80s which I believe to be made only in clear. These were the years when an endless variety of novelties were made, many of which were for children. Value of mug $30.00.

No. 823 – GRAPE WITH OVALS-CREAMER OF CHILD'S SET – I have never seen the remainder of the set, but no doubt they were made; creamer, clear only $45.00.

No. 2714 – TOM THUMB MUG – two views shown – HUMPTY DUMPTY on the other side. Clear nursery rhyme mug of this same era, clear only $50.00.

No. 1085 – FEEDING DEER AND DOG MUG – two views shown – clear only $50.00.

No. 2715 – FIGHTING CATS MUG – two views shown. Clear only; value $55.00. All of the above from the Sandwich Museum.

WHAT TO DO WITH A COLLECTION

Frequently at shows a person will happen along, inquire or pick up many pieces in the display, ask the price and sundry other questions and then say, "I have so much stuff, I just could not use another piece; I just love to look." Of course the glass is there for people to see and that part is all right but if you take time and question her further you probably will find that her possessions are rightly called "stuff." It generally consists of a heterogeneous group of pieces, unrelated in design or purpose, of questionable age and quality and condition, bought simply on the basis of the price tag. Frequently I hear a dealer say, "I just can't sell pattern glass, I have a large stock of it." Time was when I used to investigate these places and I could readily see why they could not sell it. Now pattern glass sells in every part of our country and Canada.

One never outgrows her wants and needs for old glass. My stock is never displayed in my home; I use three services in three patterns and they are kept in closed pine cases, built in, so my room does not look like a shop room. I'm still, after forty years of collecting, finding things to add to them. I need more primitives and Bennington ware for serving in our summer house (a converted garage), more old glass for grandchildren's collection, I could find possibilities for another century.

What can one do when she wakes up and finds her novice days of collecting left her with a collection of odd spooners, some of them stained, cakestands too small to hold a cake of any size, and odd small items too small for serving much of anything? Fill them with a few flowers, from your own garden, fruits or a fall bouquet of wayside weeds, grasses or pods and give them to a sick friend. Stained glass may be used for flowers and the discoloration does not show when there is water or sand in the container. But learn your lesson and collect with a purpose, hereafter.

If one lives in an apartment which is limited in space, she will have to collect small items, but do not scatter them; group them in interesting, related numbers. A nice idea is to use a certain color and hold to it for an accent color for an apartment.

2202
Scrambled Wheels Mug

2219
Brass Nailhead Mug

800
Small Flowered Tulips Mug

378
Short Loops Mug

839
Garden of Eden Mug

1218
Windmill Scene Mug
2 Views

1182
Little Buttercup Mug

No. 2202 – SCRAMBLED WHEELS MUG – Another of the odd mugs; that is, it belongs to no pattern, value $18.00 – 20.00.

No. 2219 – BRASS NAILHEAD MUG – Another odd geometric mug; *opalescent $55.00; with saucer, 100% more.*

No. 300 – SMALL TULIP WITH RIBS MUG – This mug belongs to a previously listed pattern of which there is a full sized table setting. Clear, value $45.00.

No. 378 – SHORT LOOPS MUG – Another mug part of a listed pattern of which there is a full sized table setting. Clear, value $50.00; *cobalt $200.00. One of the Sandwich toys.*

No. 839 – GARDEN OF EDEN OR LOTUS AND SERPENT MUG – Another one which is part of a well known pattern. Clear only, value $50.00. Above on this page from Sandwich Museum.

No. 1218 – WINDMILL SCENE – two views shown. Mug only, clear, value $50.00.

No. 1182 – LITTLE BUTTERCUP – Shown in my Booklet 6. Odd mug, from a scene in Gilbert and Sullivan's *The Pirates of Penzance* which came out first in 1878, the mug probably followed in the early 80s. It is made in the same technique as the "hard to photograph" Cupid and Psyche. Clear only; value $65.00.

STATE LOYALTY

I admire loyalty to one's own hearthside. I do not think it is loyalty to speculate and pay outlandish prices for a glass simply because it was made in my own state. Indiana made some beautiful glass, the Holly Amber deserves high prices; Iowa City made some fine glass, the motto plates, Horse Cat and Rabbit, etc., and several others, but why Austrian or Tepee have any special value just because one was made in Indiana and the other at Iowa City is beyond me. When I think of all the beautiful wares produced at Pittsburgh; at Sandwich, at Portland, I can't help but feel something is wrong in the scheme of things. Last year an intelligent collector, a physician, from an Iowa city called me long distance. "What's the matter with your Illinois dealers; one offered me a punch bowl in pink slag for $10,000.00." I explained that they did not know any better, they went hog wild when they found a piece of that. That's pure speculation.

Just this week I had a long distance call from a dealer in Quebec, Canada, who informed me he had refused $1,000.00 for a bowl and six sauces in Holly Amber and wanted to know what he could get and where. I told him that was glass under speculation, and I answered no telephone queries anyhow, so I could not help him. But this gives you an idea how things are running. Speculation considers no value — it's "what can I get." I can't see merchandising fine arts that way.

1000
Birds and Harp Mug
Two Views

736
Star and Ivy Cup

820
Ribbed Leaves Mug

1166
By Jingo Mug

2720
Our Boy Jester on Pig Mug

1034
Heron and Peacock

1221
Plain Monkey

No. 1000 – BIRD AND HARP – Two views shown, odd mug, clear only, value $45.00.

No. 2720 – OUR BOY-JESTER ON PIG – Odd clear mug, value $55.00. This and one above from the Sandwich Museum.

No. 1166 – BY JINGO MUG – Shown in my Booklet No. 2. Clear, odd mug, value $65.00.

No. 1034 – HERON AND PEACOCK MUG – Odd mug from Sandwich Museum. Clear $45.00; blue $65.00.

No. 1221 – PLAIN MONKEY – Called plain to distinguish him from the well known Monkey pattern to which he does not belong; that pattern has added detail of palm trees. Odd mug in clear only, value $75.00. This fellow lives in the Sandwich Museum. *Rare in deep amethyst $250.00.*

No. 820 – RIBBED LEAVES – Odd mug. From the picture, one might deduce this was a relative of the early flint ribbed patterns, but it is not. It is a contemporary, of the other, a non-flint of the 80s, in clear, value $22.00. At the Sandwich Museum.

No. 736 – STAR AND IVY – Shown is the cup of a child's cup and saucer, saucer has a plain center, rim is border of leaves with single row of pointed hobs at both edges. Value of cup and saucer $45.00; cup alone $25.00.

All of these cups and mugs are very popular at present; many are being used for serving liquid refreshments, some fit into collections of humor in glass, many are ideal for children; and in these days of small quarters small objects are much in demand. These are moderate in price, another happy consideration.

A TRUE FABLE

Years ago, when I was a dealer in a general line, I bought most of the contents of one of the fine old homes of my community. This even included family heirlooms and treasures, the breakup of the home was due to the present occupant's love for Jon Barleycorn. They sold pieces to me, bit by bit, to get money to spend on their favorite pastime. At last there was nothing old left but a set of Victorian furniture, so terrible, with huge carved lions among diverse other embellishments that I could not use it.

Several years passed, Mrs. Newly Rich moved into our quiet suburban street. I had side stepped invitations to see her home, because the thousands she had spent on the grounds was the talk of the community, the place was ruined. Marble terraces, phony animals, fountains, etc., nothing was omitted. One day the boom lowered, I had to go to our church group meeting there. I did. There in its pristine glory, shining within an inch of its life and upholstered in shocking pink velvet were my old friends, the lions. Dear Mrs. Newly Rich, with the heart of gold, confided, "I know you'll love my antique furniture. You know Bill _____, he let me have it for $8,000.00, because I love old things so."

The dear lady has since left our town so I can now share this priceless story; I believe it has a moral. I've warned you to watch out for dealers who treat you specially because _____ etc. Run, daughter, run, the Indians are coming, is my warning.

1248
Nursery Tales

825
Wee Branches—Child's Set

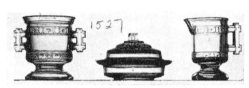

1527
Two Band Child's Set

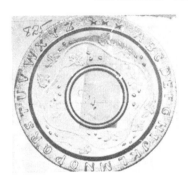

825
Butter Base

825
Creamer—Sugar

2719
Child's Number Plate

595
Stippled Diamond Child's Butter

1246
Acorn—Childs Butter Dish

No. 1248 – NURSERY TALES – In Kamm Bk. 3-63, the author states this set was made in Indiana in the 1920s according to the information she heard. I find, after I gave the same information regarding it in my Booklet No. 6, that this is probably not the case. It seems to be more a product of Pennsylvania in the 80s. It is made in the child's four piece set and in the little punch bowl with punch cups in clear and milk white. Set of four pieces in clear $425.00.

No. 825 – WEE BRANCHES – Altogether charming, previously unlisted, child's set of the 80s. This one is most unusual in that it has the alphabet around the rim of the butter (pictured). Four piece set $275.00 – 325.00.

No. 1527 – TWO BAND CHILD'S SET – Pattern described elsewhere in these pages as this pattern was made in full sized set, also and plate is shown. Value, creamer $40.00; covered butter $65.00; covered sugar $65.00; spooner $48.00.

No. 2719 – CHILD'S NUMBER PLATE – Tiny, 5" plate, in clear, probably of the 80s, seldom seen. Value $35.00.

No. 1246 – ACORN-CHILD'S BUTTER DISH – Evidently part of set. Butter $250.00.

No. 595 – STIPPLED DIAMOND-BUTTER DISH CHILD'S SET – Previously unlisted. Pattern like Stippled Forget-me-not without the blossoms. Values same as above set.

CAUSE OF PRICE CHANGE

Of course, demand is the one element which causes rise of a sudden nature in the price of glass. What causes a sudden demand? It is generally started by a magazine article in one of the cheaper magazines. Take a point in question the pattern, Manhattan, made originally in 1902 and in the shops quite recently, and not E.A.P.G. was written up in one of the cheaper magazines. Customers asked for it, dealers stocked it, prices rose. Here it was the cheapest of modern glass bringing the price of E.A.P.G.

If you note, dealers automatically divide themselves into classes; the better dealer does not handle nor recommend this type of merchandise. His merchandise does not fluctuate so much in price, he does not follow fad collecting.

You will find your long time best buy in the shop of the well informed dealer. If you survey all the publications in the field for the past twenty-five years, you will find there has been very little change in the items advertised. This is not true of the cheaper publications and the cheaper shops. It was Victorian novelties, and furniture, colored glass, art glass, Indiana and Iowa City glass, now it's speculation on specific patterns also. Later, when price bubbles burst, the collector finds he would have been better off to have been more conservative. Sometimes it pays to be "a square."

1234
Elaine or Little Red Riding Hood

2718
Hey Diddle Plate

1244
Deer ABC Plate

2716
Hex Center ABC Plate

1243
Stork ABC Plate

1245
Emma ABC Plate

1286
Covered Sugar
Child's Liberty Bell

1287
Liberty Bell Novelty

No. 1234 – ELAINE TRAY-LITTLE RED RIDING HOOD – Elaine was "the lily maid of Astolat" whose hopeless love for Sir Lancelot is one of the tales of the knights of the Round Table. She was a maiden of at least sixteen summers, so I prefer the second title as this is the picture of a child. The plate is a product of the Iowa City Glass Co., which operated for only about a year in the early 80s, but whose products are eagerly sought by a certain group of collectors, many natives of the lovely corn state. This plate comes with a plain border with the medallion handles such as are on their other plates. Their plates with mottoes, "Be virtuous," etc., are about their finest product. This plate $75.00. From Sandwich Museum.

No. 2718 – HEY DIDDLE DIDDLE PLATE – Child's nursery rhyme plate of the early 1900s. The border of the plate is very similar in technique to the McKinley plate. Value $85.00.

No. 1245 – EMMA A.B.C. PLATE – Made by Bryce, Higbee of Pittsburgh, Pa.; has been found listed in 1893 catalog to be sold at ten cents each. Clear $45.00; amber $60.00; blue $75.00. Reproduced.

No. 1243 – STORK A.B.C. PLATE – From Sandwich Museum. A rare one of the alphabet plates, all of which are in demand by collectors of them. Clear $75.00.

No. 1244 – DEER A.B.C. PLATE – Another scarce one from the Sandwich Museum. Clear $80.00.

No. 2716 – HEXAGONAL CENTER A.B.C. PLATE – Plate of the early 90s; more plentiful than some of the others. It has been reproduced, probably the old mold was handy. Value $65.00.

No. 1287 – LIBERTY BELL NOVELTY – The Liberty Bell has been used many times as a novelty. When the Liberty Bell pattern was produced at the Centennial Exposition in Philadelphia in 1876, a bell similar to one shown was made by Gillinder and Co., however, it had a little metal top for hanging. The bell shown was made for the St. Louis Exposition in 1903. A Chicago bank produced a glass bell bank in the 30s; candy containers were made as bells. Bell shown $45.00; bell of 1876 $95.00.

No. 1286 – CHILD'S SET-LIBERTY BELL-COVERED SUGAR SHOWN – Sugar is 3½" tall to top of finial. On the opposite side are the words, "100 years ago." Values: sugar $100.00; spooner $140.00; creamer $110.00; covered butter $110.00. *(Child's spooner is sometimes sold as a toothpick — not a form of the era.)*

Note: There are reproductions of alphabet plates in clear and color not originally made.

WHEN IS A REPRODUCTION NOT A REPRODUCTION?

A reproduction is not a reproduction when it is not like the piece which it is made to imitate. For instance, I said in my first book that HOLLY AMBER could not be imitated, that is, the process of obtaining that color died with the inventor of it. A toothpick is out, but it is not the color of the original pattern; it is a sickish green which should fool no one; the beautiful rich warm tone of the original is entirely lacking. I ordered a Comet sugar bowl by mail; in came a covered sugar in the pattern but in an entirely different shape; this one had a square base and was lime glass, whereas the original Comet was flint. Neither of these are reproductions. Again it's a case of degree judgment, of discrimination, all things which experience should bring. I might add that thoughtful reading helps greatly, too.

1042
Alligator Toothpick

1072
Bird Toothpick

1073
Bird Mustard

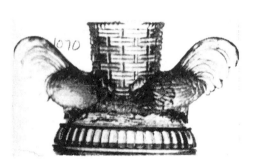

1070
Two Roosters Toothpick

1045
Rooster Head Toothpick

1066
Kitten Toothpick

2543
D & B Hat Toothpick

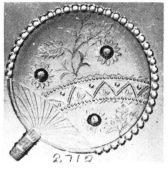

2712
Fan Plate

1201
Baby Heads Knife Rest

No. 1042 – ALLIGATOR TOOTHPICK – L. 186. Another one from the Sandwich Museum. Scarce and unusual; value $95.00.

No. 1072 – BIRD TOOTHPICK HOLDER – L. 186 calls this chicken, but if you see it in the Sandwich Museum I believe you will agree it looks more like a bird. Also scarce; clear $60.00.

No. 1073 – BIRD AND CHERRY MUSTARD – L. 186. Another from the same museum, clear, scarce, value $75.00.

No. 1070 – TWO ROOSTERS MATCH OR TOOTH-PICK HOLDER – L. 186 calls it a match holder; it is not important, probably they were used for both but their matches were the large wooden variety and I do not believe one of these quite small holders would have held many. There were numerous metal and wooden match holders. Two Roosters, clear $65.00.

No. 2543 – DAILY AND BUTTON HAT TOOTHPICK – In clear and colors, made in great quantities all through the 80s and now the shops are flooded with reproductions. In fact, most of those which I see are new. Clear $15.00; canary $40.00; amber $25.00; green or blue $25.00. From the Sandwich Museum.

No. 1066 – KITTEN ON PILLOW – L.V. 105. A scarce Daisy and Button novelty toothpick which I've never seen reproduced. From the Sandwich Museum. clear, very scarce $95.00.

No. 1201 – BABY'S HEAD KNIFE REST – Heretofore unlisted. This one in the Sandwich Museum. A picture of one of these was sent to me from California but up to that time I had never seen it. There are some who think it is a member of the Baby Face family but I do not, because the heads are entirely different. I believe it's just another serving novelty of this Victorian period. Value $55.00.

No. 1045 – ROOSTER TOOTHPICK – L. 186 shows the salt shaker with a screw top, so this is probably the toothpick. Clear, value $75.00.

No. 2712 – FAN TRAY – A very pretty little 6" card tray, clear, of the 80s, from the collection of the Willard Melvilles in Wisconsin. Value $15.00. (Note: Part of the Japanese or Grace pattern. Found in clear $40.00; amber $30.00; and blue $60.00.)

REPRODUCED PATTERNS

Daisy and Button. Many forms in colors — hats, fans, butter chips, goblets, tumblers; Heavy Panelled Grape, all forms; Moon and Star, was never made in colors shown now; Baltimore Pear; Priscilla, was never made in colors shown now; Pleat and Panel, goblets, plate; Rose in Snow, clear and colors; Panelled Thistle, all; King's Crown and Ruby Thumbprint; Red Block; Thousand Eye, clear and colored; Strawberry and Currant, goblet not made in color; Actress, goblet and pickle dish not made in colors originally; Bird with Cherry in Beak, all colors; Hobnail, clear and colored goblets, master salts in colors; Star Dewdrop, large plates, footed salts and footed sauces in colors; Inverted Thumbprint, colored goblets, tumblers, cruets and water pitcher; Diamond Quilted goblets in all colors; Beaded Grape, clear and green, especially hard to find goblet, plates; Cabbage Rose Goblet; Shell and Tassel goblet; Horn of Plenty goblet lamp; 101 goblet; Two Panel goblet, colors; Panelled Daisy goblet; Crystal Wedding goblet and compote by some mistake the fake I keep for comparison was pictured in my Book 1; Morning Glory goblet and wine, I've seen goblet listed as bargain $18.00, a real one would bring $1,000.00 now; Basketweave goblets, colors; Deer and Pine Tree goblets; Stippled Star, clear and colors; Cherry goblet; Frosted Circle goblet; Girl with Fan goblet; Jewel with Dewdrop goblet; Emerald Green Herringbone goblets and plates; Lacy Dewdrop goblets and plates; New England Pineapple goblets; "Would Be" holly amber toothpick.

Remember no listing can be infallible; new ones come out which one may not have seen. No text can keep up to the very last word. I never give the point of variance, for that is just what the fakers want; they quickly correct the published points of variance. I receive many letters telling me of a noticeable difference between what they have and one they have just seen, if you read Mr. Allen's article on Egyptian, here you will see the great number of differences which may exist in the same authentic pattern. How is one to know. If I put a new piece on a shelf among my old glass it shrieks at me; some may not have this glass sense, if you have, it will guide you. A keen sense of color is a fine guide on colored fakes, not that all old ones are the same shade of the color; they are not, but there is a difference between the old glass color and the new.

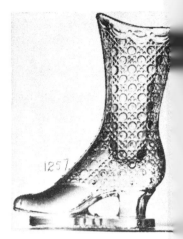

2710
Dog and Pail Toothpick

2706
Dog and Tree
Toothpick

1169
Rabbit Toothpick

1257
High Button Shoe

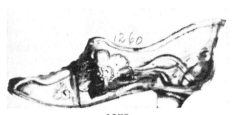

1260
Bow

1261
D & B Oxford Plain

1258
Blossom Oxford

1170
Turtle

1229
Rooster

No. 1170 – TURTLE BUTTER – K. Bk. 8-129 – L. 186. This handsome fellow is the butter to a child's toy set called The Menagerie, made by Bryce Higbee of Pennsylvania in the mid 80s. The sugar was the bear below (they made another bear like him which was a mustard), the creamer was the owl here and an upright fish was the spooner. These three pieces live in the Sandwich Museum. Bear $250.00; fish $100.00; owl $100.00; turtle, rare $700.00 – 800.00. Color add 50%.

No. 2706 – DOG AND TREE TOOTHPICK – Another novelty from the Museum at Sandwich. It does not look like a dog to me, but I'm told that is what it is. Clear only $45.00.

No. 1169 – RABBIT MATCH OR TOOTHPICK HOLDER – L. 186. Another Victorian novelty from the Sandwich Museum; clear only. Small wonder these are scarce, no one would want to give up such a nice pet bunny. Clear only $75.00.

No. 1257 – HIGH BUTTON SHOE-CANE – This clear one is at the Sandwich Museum; it is more plentiful and comes in colors; clear $45.00; amber $50.00; blue $55.00. At times, these shoes are found with shoe ads on the soles; this adds to, rather than detracts from, their value.

No. 1260 – BOW OXFORD – Another from the same museum. Comes in clear and colors; clear $30.00; amber $35.00; canary $50.00; blue $45.00.

No. 1261 – DAISY AND BUTTON OXFORD – Another from the Sandwich Museum. Clear and colored. Same values as the one above. Most of them one sees are reproductions. At times we see them with the patent date on the sole which is a protection.

No. 1258 – BLOSSOM SLIPPER – Slipper of the early 90s, flowers were originally painted. Quite scarce. Clear only $50.00.

No. 2710 – DOG AND PAIL MATCH OR TOOTH-PICK HOLDER – Another scarce novelty from the Sandwich Museum. Clear only; value $65.00.

No. 1249 – BUTTER DISH-CHILD'S ROOSTER SET – At first sight I thought this was not the original cover but after seeing another and the sugar I was convinced it was. Previously unlisted. Covered butter $150.00; covered sugar $175.00; creamer $140.00; spooner $150.00; complete set $600.00 – 700.00.

1237
Pretty Maid Toothpick

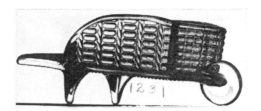

1231
Indented Ovals Wheelbarrow

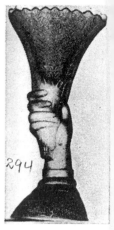

1294
Hand Vase

1240
Cart Salt

1252
Engine

1030
Dog Medallion Child's Cup

1239
Horse Drawn Cart Toothpick

1096
Lion's Head Child's Cup

No. 1237 – PRETTY MAID TOOTHPICK – This is 5" tall; I've seen it only in clear. These may have been for matches but in the 80s, and early 90s, when most of these novelties were made, it was the height of style to serve toothpicks. Value $75.00.

No. 1294 –HAND VASE – L.V. 106. Another Victorian novelty, the kind of which their rooms were crowded. Vase has vertical fern fronds, small, clear and frosted, value $55.00. This runs into more money because it is sought by "Hand" collectors.

No. 1252 – ENGINE CANDY CONTAINER – Here is another late glass which is worth saving; the present coming generation is not familiar with this type of engine which was so important in its day. A "natural" for little boys; value $65.00.

No. 1231 – INDENTED OVALS WHEELBARROW – Not previously listed. There is a wheelbarrow in the pattern Barley. *Most scholars don't believe the so called Barley wheelbarrow is truly a part of the Barley pattern. Merely an individual piece that resembles the pattern. Clear only; value $75.00 – 100.00. The Greentown wheelbarrow is much sought after, but has been reproduced.*

No. 1239 – HORSE DRAWN CART TOOTHPICK – Another reminder of the way things were. Clear only; value $50.00. Now reproduced.

No.. 1030 – DOG MEDALLION – Child's cup and saucer. Saucer has dog's head in center. Clear cup and saucer $75.00; blue $85.00.

NO. 1240 – CART MASTER SALT – Clear, non-flint; value $45.00.

No. 1096 – LION'S HEAD CUP AND SAUCER – Part of child's set; saucer has full length lion stretched out in the center. Clear $95.00.

Due to small living quarters today, small objects are much in demand, hence all of these are fast disappearing from the shops. While some are late, they make a fine door to the world of old things for children especially.

WHAT GRANDMA HAD

Frequently, at shows, dealers, especially those whose stock contains many late items, will hear folks say, "Grandma had that, and we threw it out." At times, the dealer retorts facetiously, "We kept this and threw out Grandma." Some even have signs supposed to be humorous stating this.

Many times I receive letters from sincere people who have received from grandma one of these late patterns which I have called "not recommended," in my book and pleas for advice. Keep it by all means; it is old glass, but not E.A.P.G. and you should remember that when you are buying it and are paying for it. In referring to it, remember you do not have a collection of antiques, but family tradition is above all, worthwhile, it and the right kind of family pride are closely related — pride in an unblemished name, an honorable reputation. We don't need to go overboard and follow the Chinese into ancestor worship but our grandparents are a rather good old American institution, ask any youngster!

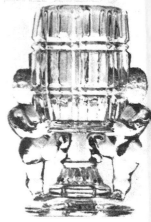

2709
Three Dolphins

2708
Dog Holding Bowl
Match

2711
Saddle Toothpick

1167
Cherub
Novelty Toothpick

2722
Monkey Match

1027
Swan and Cart Salt

1040
Frog Toothpick

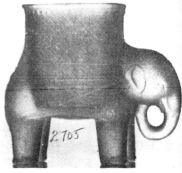

2707
Reclining Dog Salt

503
Crown Jewel Inkwell

2705
Fancy Elephant Toothpick

No. 2709 – THREE DOLPHINS MATCH OR TOOTH-PICK HOLDER – L. 186 calls it simply DOLPHIN but as it does not belong to the earlier family by that name, I've added a word. The one shown is amber and is in the Sandwich Museum; value clear $50.00; amber $60.00; if there is a blue one it would be worth $70.00. L.V. 104 shows this same thing with a plain stem with no dolphins, value $30.00.

No. 2708 – DOG HOLDING BOWL SALT – L. 127. Also in the Sandwich Museum; a scarce novelty; clear stippled glass. *Metz erred. This is not a salt, but a child's sugar, missing its lid, from the Standing Lamb pattern. Complete about $700.00.*

No. 2711 – SADDLE TOOTHPICK OR MATCH HOLDER – L. 127. Another scarce one in amber in the Sandwich Museum. Value $95.00.

No. 1167 – CHERUB TOOTHPICK OR MATCH HOLDER – L. 186. Shown in my Booklet No. 2. There is also a related perfume bottle, in which these same cherubs hold a swirled bottle. These Victorian novelties are really not E.A.P.G. but their whimsey relates them to it; they were produced at the time of some of the later patterns and they fit in nicely with it. Either toothpick or vase $35.00. Clear only. Vase now reproduced.

No. 1027 – SWAN DRAWING CART SALT – L. 186. This salt and toothpick above are from the Sandwich Museum; 4" long, clear only; value $65.00.

No. 2722 – MONKEY HEAD-DARWIN TOOTHPICK OR MATCH HOLDER – L.V. 105. Made by Richards and Hartley in Pennsylvania and called by them, Darwin. Possibly, this was just after the death of the scientist in 1882. Clear stippled glass, value $50.00.

No. 2705 – FANCY ELEPHANT TOOTHPICK – L. 127. This finely dressed elephant is in amber glass in the Sandwich Museum. Value, clear $95.00; amber $110.00.

No. 1040 – FROG TOOTHPICK – L. 127. Another match or toothpick holder, this one in clear glass from the same museum. I believe this one certainly typifies the whimsey of which I spoke. Value, clear $95.00.

No. 503 – CROWN JEWEL INK WELL – Also called CHANDELIER – Part of a pattern that couldn't be put in another part of book with remainder of the pattern where it belonged. Value $65.00; top is hard rubber.

No. 2707 – RECLINING DOG SALT – L. 186. From the sandwich Museum. Clear, non-flint, value $75.00.

LET US PUNCTURE ANOTHER BUBBLE

This bubble is going to be hard to prick because its hide has been toughened by long usage. One sees a pontil mark and says to herself, "Blown"; even, it is seen in pattern glass ads. Has it ever occurred to the reader that this is an anachronism; Pattern glass is a pressed product which followed the blown glass. The answer is that in the early days of pressing glass, the pontil rod was frequently used to hold the goblet as it was removed from the mold for finishing touches. It does signify early manufacture. This may help those who have wondered. If you are interested in the type of glass which preceded the pattern ware and which was blown into molds I suggest you read Ruth Webb Lee's *Victorian Glass* and *American Glass and Two Hundred Years of Blown Glass* by McKearin. This glass went by many names, first Stoddard, then insufflated, molded, blown molded, three mold blown. Here is where the mistaken idea came that mold marks mean something in pattern glass. Here they mean nothing.

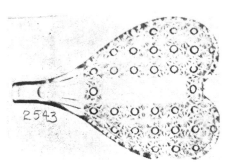

2543
D & B Heart Shaped Tray

2543
D & B Dustpan

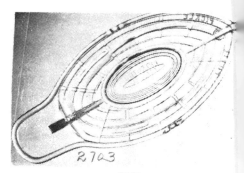

2703
Patented Pickle Dish

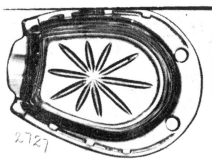

2727
Natural Horseshoe Salt

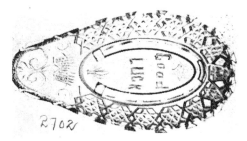

2702
Natural Horseshoe Pickle

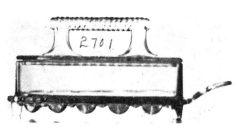

2701
Flat Iron Covered Dish
Two Views

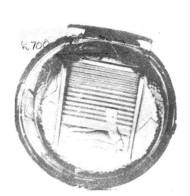

2700
Wash Tub Open Soap Dish
Two Views

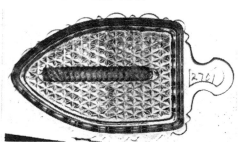

No. 2727 – NATURALISTIC HORSESHOE SALT – Called Naturalistic to distinguish it from the other two patterns based on the horseshoe motif. This is an odd novelty salt, from the Sandwich Museum; clear only, value $20.00.

No. 2543 – HEART SHAPED DAISY AND BUTTON TRAY – Novelty tray in this pattern in the shape of one of the old rounded fans. This tray had the name, "Lily," in the center although it possibly came with other names also. The other fan shaped trays in this pattern are copiously reproduced, not so this one. Value is clear $25.00; canary $50.00; amber $30.00; in blue $35.00.

No. 2543 – DAISY AND BUTTON DUST PAN TRAY – Another tray on this pattern which has not been reproduced to date. Clear $20.00; canary $35.00; amber $25.00; blue $30.00. *Reproduced.*

No. 2701 – FLAT IRON COVERED DISH – (side and top view shown). Clear $40.00; canary $85.00; amber $50.00; blue $75.00. Now reproduced.

No. 2700 – WASH TUB SOAP DISH – two views shown. This will certainly be a novelty to the coming generation. A really different ash tray for the coffee table. Clear $65.00; canary $100.00; amber $70.00; blue $75.00.

No. 2703 – PATENTED PICKLE DISH – Clear, labeled, "Pickles," and date, "1874." How would one dare to serve anything else in a dish so plainly labeled? Victorian over zealousness to detail shown here in another form; one must be most formal and prim. Value $25.00.

No. 2702 – REAL HORSESHOE TRAY – Another pickle or relish dish although I suppose one might even serve celery or candies in this as it is not labeled. Clear, of the 80s. Value $25.00.

HOW TO LURE HUSBANDS TO COLLECTING TRIPS

My own husband was not keen to go all the way east to visit the Sandwich Museum, but then there was the Baseball Museum at Cooperstown, New York. Would he like to visit that? You just know he would. In Cooperstown is a fine museum of primitives in the old Fennimore Cooper home and then there is the Farmer's Museum, a delight to any one, who ever saw a farm, needless to say it delighted my husband who was raised on one. His mood was so good that the journey to Sandwich was a breeze. After his death I had to inveigle my son to take the same trip; he's a boating enthusiast, so Mystic, Connecticut, with that last word in maritime museums was the bait and did it work. You too, glass collectors will love these other museums — to walk on the cobblestone streets of Mystic is fun, I loved it.

NOT OLD
Pinwheels

Not Old-Lined Hob

Lined Hob—New
Iob with Lined Bands

Panelled Goblet
Warning
Not E.A.P.C.

Starburst

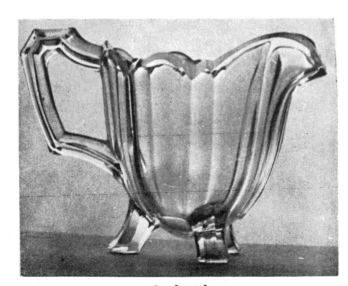

Quadruped

Swirl and Diamond

NO! NO! A THOUSAND TIMES NO!

Far be it from me to dictate to any collector what he should collect; I'm not out to reform the "I know what I like cult," besides, as one dealer flaunts, "Junk can be jaunty." I've seen some very clever arrangements made with pieces which I had previously considered hopeless. However, I believe people should buy with their eyes open and a tight hand on their wallets and realize that they are not buying E.A.P.G. and that there is little future in this type of merchandise; prices should be made accordingly. You do not find this type of ware in the stock of first class dealers, nor in the advertising columns of our fine magazine on antiques. It can be used as one yardstick by which to judge the quality of a shop. Occasionally a piece slips into a museum as part of a collection. At one time, Mrs. Kamm gave as one reason for collecting some of this late ware, the fact that it was not reproduced. This is no longer true; many of the horrible imitation cut glass patterns are advertised in our home magazines as, "Reproductions of Early American Pattern Glass — made from original molds." The patterns are so new that old molds are frequently found in usable condition; few advertising agency copy writers have any knowledge of this subject.

NOTE: I am not assigning these pattern numbers as they are not E.A.P.G.

SWIRL AND DIAMOND – K. Bk. 4-94. None of the flavor of old glass.

LINED HOBNAIL – I warned of this in my Booklet No. 4. K. Bk. 7-24 calls it HOBNAIL WITH LINED BAND. Mil. Bk. 2-5 calls it FLATTENED HOBNAIL-BANDED. I remember when this struck the dime stores about thirty-five years ago. A far cry from the old Hobnail.

STARBURST – Mil. Bk. 2-104–K. Bk. 5-36 calls it STAR-LYTE. No possible resemblance to old glass.

SPINNER DAISY – Mil. Bk. 2-86. This is the type of imitation cut glass which is entirely beyond the pale.

PINWHEELS – K. Bk. 1-100. Another of the type of the one above. Enough said.

QUADRUPED – K. Bk. 2-117 – When one sees this she feels she might walk into Mr. Woolworth's and find a duplicate today.

PANELLED GOBLET – I've seen this goblet sold as a Loop goblet, as Flute goblet, as Panelled goblet. It is, I fear, not American, for I've seen it most frequently among stocks containing many imports. It is very thin, flint and I believe quite recent also. It has none of the characteristics of E.A.P.G.

OTHER PITFALLS BESIDES REPRODUCTIONS

There are other tricks which some dealers employ besides selling reproductions; sometimes the mistakes are due to lack of knowledge. Some will put any cover on any base which it will fit, regardless of whether or not it is the pattern to which it belongs. To match this we have the perfectionist collector who will not accept a cover, albeit the original one if it does not fit with hair line precision. Glass, at times, could become very slightly misshapen in removal from the mold and the two parts will not have the modern, "electric eye measured precision" of some modern processes. I had a customer who rejected a blue milk glass piece because base and cover were very slightly different in shade. Covers and bases can be run from two batches and again, they did not have the testing we have. If you are this type of person, you don't belong in the antique collecting fraternity. One of the trials of my existence this summer, is a yard man who wanted to trim all my shrubs into perfect spheres, and plant my flowers in symmetrical straight rows. Can you imagine what the world would have been, had our Creator used that plan all over? Needless to say, informed, reliable dealers spend little time with this kind of collector; "we got them on our list."

MORE NO! NO'S!
(Not Pictured)

SILVER ANNIVERSARY – Mil. 62. This is listed as of the 80s, whereas 1920 would more nearly hit it. It is decorated with that silver trim still found in the stores. No resemblance to old glass. *Cornflower, emerald green w/gold.*

PANELLED 44 – Mil. Bk. 2-72 says its of the 80s. It is a far cry from old glass, gilt top, purple trim, definitely not E.A.P.G., more likely 1928. Reverse 44.

DIAMOND POINT-MILK WHITE – Mil. Bk. 2-72 says it's of the 1900s. It's not Diamond Point and as for the date it is still in the gift shops. Never was an old one like it.

ZIG-ZAG BLOCK – Mil. Bk. 2-106 dates this goblet in the 70s as it is rather heavy. It is suspiciously like a very popular modern pattern which one of our large glass firms has been issuing for the past 30 years. *Fostoria American.*

STIPPLED BELLFLOWER – Mil. B. 2-101. This gay deceiver takes a fairly respectable picture, but he will fool no one once you see him. No possible member of the Bellflower family and not E.A.P.G., possibly foreign.

ENGLISH HOBNAIL WITH FLOWER BAND – My notes on this one are incomplete, but somewhere along the line I've found this one listed and I've pictured him from one of the collections, some of which tried to include one of every one listed and consequently were not selective. This is another factor one must remember when visiting museums. I've by no means shown all of those listed in the different books which are unworthy of listing, but I've tried to give a sample of what is meant by E.A.P.G.

WARNING!

Some people think that because an article appears in a magazine in which they have faith, that it is necessarily all right. Such is not the case. There is no magazine published today that could possibly guarantee or which does guarantee this. Knowingly, they would not disappoint you, but policing this field takes an expert working full time, just at that; price would be prohibitive; ads could not be surveyed in time.

REFERENCE BOOKS

When my first book was issued, one reviewer thought he found many errors in references to plate and page numbers of other text. A book containing a check list of patterns was issued shortly and as I checked it, I found my plate numbers did not agree. To my surprise, I found different issues of the books had differing plate numbers and there was where all our difficulty had been. So I'm listing the issues from which the plate numbers I used were taken.

Early American Pressed Glass – Handbook – Ruth Webb Lee – 13th printing.

Early American Pattern Glass – Ruth Webb Lee – the founder of the intensive listing of patterns.

Lee – *Victorian Glass* – Handbook – Fourth Printing.

Victorian Glass – Ruth Webb Lee – Much glass information found since Mrs. Lee's death.

Goblets – S.T. Millard – Book I – First Printing. Dr. Millard found many new patterns.

Goblets – Book 2 – S.T. Millard – Second Edition.

Thumbnail Sketches – J. Stanley Bothers, Jr.

Kamm – *Early American Pattern Glass Pitchers* – Books 1 – 8. All first editions.

Fakes and Reproductions – Ruth Webb Lee – Remember, the author has been dead several years, changes have been made on many fakes and many new ones are out. This book is good foundation knowledge. Mrs. Lee fought fakes every moment of her life.

The American Story Recorded in Glass – Tracy H. Marsh. Historical glass.

Lore of Our Land Pictured in Glass – Bessie M. Lindsey – Vol. 1 and 2. I believe now out of print.

Cambridge Glass – Lura Woodside Watkins – Story of the New England Glass Co.

Early Canadian Glass – Gerald Stevens.

Portland Glass – Frank H. Swan – A few copies of this are still for sale by his niece, Miss Marion Dana, 45 Thomas St., Portland, Me.

Please do not write me to ask where you can buy these books, your book store can find many for you and many are advertised in your magazines. Many can be seen in your library. If you are interested in Sandwich glass, Ruth Webb Lee wrote a good book on that, if you collect cup plates, there are books on that, books on art glass, etc. Books by specialists are the best. One cannot cover all angles thoroughly and well.

INDEX

ARTICLE INDEX

Schroeder's
ANTIQUES
Price Guide

. . . is the #1 bestselling antiques & collectibles value guide on the market today, and here's why . . .

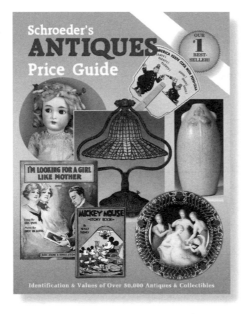

Identification & Values of Over 50,000 Antiques & Collectibles

8½ x 11 • 608 Pgs. • PB • $12.95

• *More than 300 advisors, well-known dealers, and top-notch collectors work together with our editors to bring you accurate information regarding pricing and identification.*

• *More than 45,000 items in almost 500 categories are listed along with hundreds of sharp original photos that illustrate not only the rare and unusual, but the common, popular collectibles as well.*

• *Each large close-up shot shows important details clearly. Every subject is represented with histories and background information, a feature not found in any of our competitors' publications.*

• *Our editors keep abreast of newly developing trends, often adding several new categories a year as the need arises.*

If it merits the interest of today's collector, you'll find it in *Schroeder's*. And you can feel confident that the information we publish is up to date and accurate. Our advisors thoroughly check each category to spot inconsistencies, listings that may not be entirely reflective of market dealings, and lines too vague to be of merit. Only the best of the lot remains for publication.

Collector Books
P.O. Box 3009
Paducah, KY 42002-3009
1-800-626-5420
www.collectorbooks.com

COLLECTOR BOOKS
A Division of Schroeder Publishing Co., Inc.